Praise f‹

"An invaluable book in such hard times, *Witchcraft Activism* really gets into the realities of what it takes to make lasting, positive change through the political machine. Whether it be grassroots activism at the local level or marching on the National Mall, David Salisbury gives us the 411 on what it takes and how to organize to make change happen. From social justice spells to self-protection wards on the picket lines, there's plenty of magic and real-world action for everyone to apply to their own activism, regardless of whether you're a practitioner of witchcraft or are just passionate to make a difference in politics."

—Tomás Prower, author of *Queer Magic:*
LGBT+ Spirituality and Culture from Around the World

"I've been a huge fan of David Salisbury as both an author and a human being for quite a while now. His work, in regards to both activism and witchcraft, is not only highly inspiring, but Salisbury is also one of the most authentic and dedicated human beings I've had the pleasure of coming across. Salisbury is neither an armchair occultist nor a keyboard warrior activist—he's someone who is always rolling up his sleeves to do the actual work both behind the scenes and on the front lines in both these areas. *Witchcraft Activism* is a masterful blend of these two areas of Salisbury's expertise and passion. The book is a fantastic and intelligent guide employing strategic tactics of using magick to create much needed social change that anyone can operate, regardless of their magickal experience or skill level."

—Mat Auryn, author *of Psychic Witch*
and blogger of *For Puck's Sake* on Patheos Pagan

"David Salisbury's *Witchcraft Activism* is clearly the produact of someone who has done the difficult, unglamorous, boots-on-the-ground work required for creating social and political change. If you want spells and magical advice, you'll find them, of course, but Salisbury's insights into everyday activism are where the book stands out."

—Michael Hughes, author of
Magic for the Resistance: Rituals and Spells for Change

"Utilizing personal and magical power to impact change is at the heart of activism. It is within the fibers of our spirits to navigate the space in between the present and the limitless future—this knowingness leads to accountability and manifestation. In *Witchcraft Activism*, David Salisbury explores the many different ways that witchcraft and activism collide and some of the fundamental steps to engaging the power of both sides to support our desired outcomes. Whether protesting in the streets, petitioning

your local politician, or working the magic on your altar, this book brings attention to the interwoven threads that enmesh our workings with our sociopolitical power."
—Crystal Blanton, author of *Shades of Ritual* and *Shades of Faith*

"Those who practice witchcraft often keenly feel the movements and actions of powers in the world, both spiritual and mundane. Naturally, more and more practitioners are being called to work their magick to protect, heal, foster, and advance their communities. More witches are becoming activists, and more are writing openly about using witchcraft as a tool for activism. One of the things that makes David Salisbury's *Witchcraft Activism* especially useful is that it addresses what is needed to become an activist and maintain the balance needed for the long road ahead. The workings, spells, exercises, protocols for planning, and so on are clear-eyed and practical, but it is the care and feeding of the activist's heart and soul that makes this book a treasure."
—Ivo Dominguez Jr., author of
Keys to Perception: A Practical Guide to Psychic Development

"*Witchcraft Activism* is an invaluable tool. David Salisbury's work is clear and easy to follow. A perfect blend of history, practical applications, and spiritual devotions, this belongs on the shelf of every magick practitioner, whether or not they are an activist . . . as well as on the shelf of every activist, whether or not they practice magick."
—Courtney Weber, author of *Brigid: History, Mystery, and Magick of the Celtic Goddess* and *The Morrigan: Celtic Goddess of Magick and Might*

"Witchcraft is inherently political; the work naturally highlights the connections between us as human beings and the world around us. In his book, David Salisbury eloquently describes how the metaphysical and physical can definitely go hand in hand to create effective social and environmental change, regardless of your path, position, or ability. This practical guide covers easy-to-understand techniques and demonstrates how to methodically apply them to a variety of situations, as well as touching on inspiring history to reflect upon. *Witchcraft Activism* is an accessible and valuable resource for building community and bringing about effective change."
—Laura Tempest Zakroff, author of
Weave the Liminal and *Sigil Witchery* and editor of
The New Aradia: A Witch's Handbook to Magical Resistance

WITCH
CRAFT
ACTIVISM

a toolkit for
magical resistance

DAVID SALISBURY

WEISER BOOKS

This edition first published in 2019 by Weiser Books, an imprint of
Red Wheel/Weiser, LLC
With offices at:
65 Parker Street, Suite 7
Newburyport, MA 01950
www.redwheelweiser.com

ISBN: 978-1-57863-657-0
Library of Congress Cataloging-in-Publication Data
available upon request.

Cover design by Kathryn Sky-Peck
Interior photos/images by David Salisbury
Interior by Steve Amarillo / Urban Design LLC
Typeset in Adobe Bembo and Insigne Civane

Printed in Canada
MAR
10 9 8 7 6 5 4 3 2 1

Contents

Introduction

It's hard to say which came first in my life: activism or magic. Being a rather unusual child (as is the nature of many magic workers), I was always hyperaware of injustice toward people, animals, and nature. Some of my earliest memories were of being bullied and then, later, seeing the bullies get bullied by others. I noticed a pattern of harm early on, where innocent people would have bad things done to them and then go on to repeat the cycle themselves. It always struck me as odd, because it didn't seem like anyone enjoyed either end of the cycle.

As for me, wishing to escape all of that pain that I couldn't solve on my own, I retreated to the safety of the natural world. In the rust-belt city of Buffalo, New York, where I grew up there wasn't a whole lot of obvious nature around, but there were some places where I found sanctuary—the shores of Lake Erie, a grove of oak trees in the corner of the little neighborhood park, and the little creek that ran alongside my road, 7th Street. On many days of solitude, nature became a teacher, friend, and guide. From nature, and the spirits inhabiting it, I learned that being othered in a rough world was not just a burden, but also an opportunity.

As I grew up, I'd find opportunities for myself and those around me through both magic and activism. Magic came into my life around the age of twelve, when I met a Wiccan priestess in my hometown who became my mentor.

I got involved in activism in a more organized way around age fifteen, when I began organizing for LGBTQ, environmental, and animal rights through groups in high school. These days, I spend my time as a professional political organizer in Washington, D.C., and help lead one of the region's most active and outspoken witchcraft traditions. You could say that I'm really in the thick of things when it comes to magic and activism.

Each thing informs the other. Through magic, I learned that I was not only responsible for myself, but for the world around me as well. I learned that if I carefully cultivated my inner power, I could create changes that made the world just ever so slightly easier to be in. Through activism, I learned how to develop the inner confidence and cunning required to make changes that actually last and remain effective. Most importantly, each thing has provided a check to the other. Activism kept me grounded and encouraged a sense of personal responsibility. Magic reminded me that even when the world seems fraught with terror and oppression, the ingenuity of the human spirit—that hidden spark of angelic fire within us all—is enough to see us through.

I truly believe that there is no separating magic from the spirit of revolution. The personal is always political, and the political is always personal.

Did you know that just one cubic inch of your bones can hold 19,000 pounds? Ounce for ounce, they're roughly five times stronger than steel. We are all stronger than we think. There is a great power in our bones and in our bodies. Magicians are often called "workers" for a reason. Nearly every tradition of the Craft teaches the importance of the body as the prime tool and impetus for magical strength, which doesn't necessarily mean physical strength. In learning magic, we train our bodies to enter different states of consciousness to connect us with other worlds. By building up the strength of the mind, we can project and manifest our desires. Our existence alone is a miraculous set of circumstances worthy of marvel. A seemingly impossible set of cosmic circumstances had to perfectly align for us to be here. Choices made by our ancestors for thousands of years crafted the DNA that makes us who we are today as individuals. Just like our bodies, the land is an inseparable source of the witch's power. Stones, roots, flowers, trees, stars, and bones have all been sources of inspiration for witches since time immemorial.

The body has also always been politicized. We may think of issues of body image, reproduction, surface sexuality, and more as relatively modern, but all of these topics are deeply embedded in human existence. There is no separating our body from politics. There is no separating witchcraft from the body. That goes for the bodies of humans and the body of this Earth itself. This power we seek to know and wield is embedded as deeply in the soil as it is in our bones.

Magic will always respond to a world in crisis. We are meant to weave together the broken fibers of humanity; the solar cloth of Bríg, the Golden Fleece, Ariadne's thread, the Red String of Fate. The political landscape of magic workers is as varied as the people, with all their views, hopes, and dreams. But where a dream most often stays a hidden secret of the mind, witchcraft is the unconquerable shout at midnight. It screams to be heard because it is the lighthouse for the voiceless.

Whether you like politics, advocacy, and civic engagement or not, you are engaging in political action when you perform and embody magical principles. Witchcraft is not a spectator sport. It is in our bodies, our communities, our lands, and our streets. We cannot separate ourselves from the world because we are the world.

In this book you won't find me critiquing various forms of magic and activism, both topics that are as widely debated as they are practiced. Instead I'll be piecing together a practical manual based on my experiences within both worlds. You'll notice that I weave together what we may think of as "the physical" with magical application, sometimes without a strong distinction between the two. This is important and intentional. I'd like you to think about one while you're doing the other, so much so that they feel as seamless and inseparable to you as a flag to its pole.

Finally, I will caution you to use your best judgment while you navigate the waters of the magical activist. There are always situations one cannot prepare for, and no book can tell you how to become a smarter leader, strategist, and worker all at once. Your lived experience from engaging with a variety of actions will ultimately be more valuable. Still, I've tried to provide the tools necessary to help you feel prepared. Whether you're a seasoned advocate or just starting out, I'm sure you'll find a trick or two in here to help you on your way.

This work can be messy, hard, stressful, and painful. It can also be rewarding beyond measure. Most of all, it is important and worth your effort. There has never been a time when the world needed our activism and our magic more. For those who feel called to bring the two together, I believe that the groundwork for miraculous change can be laid.

The Basics

Activism in Its Many Forms

When I discuss activism with people in my community, I notice two very common assumptions: either someone thinks that activism looks like a very specific thing and nothing else or that it's too many things and entirely overwhelming because of that. Of course, the real nature of activism lives somewhere in the middle. It can be simple, complicated, strategic, spontaneous, lighthearted, aggressive, done by one person, or engaged in by a whole collective. Because of the diversity of tactics and tone, people can get pretty heated up when talking about the "right way" to go about creating change. While there are certainly methods that are more effective for certain goals than others, there is a lot of room for discussion.

As with any topic that's hotly debated—and magic and activism are debated in equal measure—we can help close the gap by developing some common language and considering what we mean when we talk about different actions and when, how, and why to take them. It's important to know the basic forms so that you're ready to move when the moment strikes. I tend to break down the major forms of activism into roughly six different types. Let's look at those now.

Learning and Educating

It is easy to underestimate the value of having a conversation. In our fast-paced world of social media and texting, we consume so much information that it can be challenging to have any sort of meaningful exchange with others. When we do, we're often so focused on getting a point across that the message gets lost in the process. To start our journey into effective advocacy, we must understand the essentials of learning and educating. These concepts aren't just valuable on their own, but also dependent upon each other. You can't educate others without being willing to learn, and you can't learn if you don't know how to express your ideas back to the world.

Psychologists know that humans learn through a variety of methods and experiences. By understanding the way we learn, we can position ourselves to better absorb information and help others do the same.

Observational Learning. This is learning by seeing or sensing something directly. For example, you probably learned how to tie your shoes by seeing someone else do it first. Learning through observation is a core process within activism because we're often trying to tell stories to get people to experience or empathize with the plights of others. If you can create an experience that a person can observe well enough for it to "sink in," then your work is going to be that much more effective. In the magical principles of Hermeticism, we might relate this to the Principle of Mentalism that everything in the universe is of one mind and what we do is the result of a thought that came before the action.

Associative Learning. Connecting two or more events or situations and drawing a conclusion from those events is called associative learning. When the outdoors go from being sunny to dark suddenly in the middle of the day, we might instinctively look up to the sky in anticipation of rain. Seeing the correlation between two things helps us predict what might come next. Understanding that humans learn by association is helpful because people bring their own ideas of all kinds about what activism is when it's presented to them. Sometimes those experiences are bad, which means you'll need to retrain the person to associate your work with the positive change you're trying to bring about. In looking at our Hermetic principles, we might relate this to the Law of Correspondence: everything is connected (for good or ill) to something else. Understanding these connections grants us the extraordinary ability to rewire them in pursuit of our goals.

Cultural factors also play an enormous role in our ability to process information and learn from it. This is challenging for people doing activist work because everyone comes to the information with a huge array of cultural experiences we may know nothing about. For example, working alongside a person of color on racial justice issues is going to present a different set of experiences than working alongside a white person whether we are white or a person of color ourselves. While we can learn from both colleagues, the way we learn and what we offer in return are often going to be different. The same is true for any other number of identities, cultures, and personal backgrounds that inform how individual activists live and work.

Understanding how we learn, the next step is to actually seek out the knowledge. Of course, learning is a lifelong process that should hopefully never be complete for any of us, but we have to start somewhere. For the activist, the most vital source of information is what we can glean through listening to the communities affected. I cannot stress this enough. Listening to the people you are trying to help and ally yourself with must always be the first thing in any effort. This work is not easy and will often result in discomfort. Learning is not always fun, and it is not always invited. But we must remain constantly willing to be open to it. This is partly out of respect, but it is also crucial to the integrity of your work and to ensuring that the work is serving in the best and most welcome way possible.

Staying open to learning is only a first step; it doesn't do much good to keep it all to ourselves. One of the major roles of the activist is to educate our own communities about the issues that are important to us.

Just like learning from others, educating others requires skill, integrity, compassion, and will. We need the skills of a teacher to present the information in ways that will be best absorbed by our audience. We need integrity to ensure that what we're teaching is honest, ethical, and right. We need to educate with compassion, knowing that everyone comes to learn about issues new to them at a difference pace and from different perspectives. Without compassion, we risk having our audience shut down and block out the message entirely. Finally, we must have the will to share what we've learned and make the choice to do so. Without the will to do this work, our methods of teaching will start to look like a chore—forced and unnatural.

When educating others on an issue, try to keep the following core principles in mind:

* **Focus on the message rather than the messenger.** Unless you are part of the community being directly affected by the issue you're working on, it's important not to center efforts on yourself when you can help it. Prop up the message rather than yourself as the delivery person. This doesn't just go for discussions, but for events as well. If you're lobbying government officials, avoid anything that might sidetrack people's attention. For example, dress so that your message is the focus rather than what you are wearing. Is it fair for people to judge your message based on you as the delivery person? No. But it is the reality.

* **Choose arguments carefully.** While debate is a form of education, it can quickly turn into an argument. It's important where possible to avoid heated discussions more focused on feelings rather than facts, which often become personal. Arguments don't often result in the other person walking away considering what you've brought to the table. While it can be extremely challenging, it's better to try and be the bigger person. There are other benefits to going this route. Others observing an argument will often side with the person who remained calm and presented clear facts. They'll remember that you had the confidence to keep your cool, which could make them more interested in learning about what you have to say. It's also possible that the angry person will later regret acting rudely to someone who

kept their cool, which might cause them to reconsider the information at a later time. Finally, arguing with someone who isn't open to your message is a waste of time. That energy can be better spent doing good things elsewhere.

★ **Keep it simple.** At least at first, meet people where they are. A major problem among some progressives is the use of extremely convoluted "social justice jargon" when explaining something. People don't like to feel like they're being lectured. Humans respond better to conversations with people who they share some common ground with. If someone seems brand-new to your issue, start with the basics and work your way up from there. Remember that it might take more than a moment for the person to grasp some initial concepts. Gradually build up your level of education from there. This requires some time and commitment and isn't something you're always going to be able to do well, so be patient. Recognize that with a stranger on the street you may only be able to plant a seed of a positive connection rather than sharing your whole program all at once.

Learning and educating are tasks that will be woven into every form of activism you engage in. As you look at the different ways activists push for change, try to identify how these concepts can be put into motion.

Power of the Pen:
Petitioning and Letter-Writing

Petitioning decision-makers is one of the oldest and most cherished forms of activism in the Western world and beyond. Petitioning is an accessible way for anyone's voice to be heard. I fondly recall the first time I ever wrote a petition letter for a cause. It was a class exercise in fifth grade, and we were asked to write letters to a major beverage company concerning their use of land and water resources. I remember being fascinated with the idea that writing a letter could make the world a better place. I still hold that same fascination, and I've seen it work.

In the digital age of sending and receiving constant communications from around the globe, you might be tempted to think that writing to people, companies, and governments is not an impactful way to make a difference. But consider this: there is an understanding on Capitol Hill that a handwritten (or typed and printed) letter is as valuable as dozens of emails. Even one constituent sending an email to a legislator is noticed, too. Many legislators consider one email from a single person to represent the will of ten or more other constituents.

It's important to keep letters short and to the point, but also personal and passionate. Most of the time your letters are going to be read at least initially by the staff and interns of the elected official. Letters to companies and organizations should also be brief, as even larger companies tend to keep their customer mail exchange programs rather short. They are often just churning out reply letters based on volume, so don't be surprised if you don't get a personal response when writing to a company.

The appropriate and most effective tone of a letter or email is hotly debated in the world of advocacy. Many people say that respect and politeness are always best, that you "catch more flies with honey than vinegar." Others insist that we should always speak our mind and let our true authentic selves show up strongly in our messaging. I tend to be in the camp that considers each situation and different tones based on what one is trying to convey and achieve.

Polite letters increase the chance that the person reading it will make it all the way through and really consider what the writer is saying. Letters that feel positive in nature tend to make their way through the system with more ease, which is true in both the government and businesses. That said, I do believe there are times when a stronger approach is called for. When it comes to members of Congress, your senators and representatives should realize that you're one of the people that gave them that position and you're someone who can take it away from them as well. Notice I said "should." That unfortunately doesn't apply to every member of Congress or we'd have a much higher functioning government than we do. Regardless, showing that you mean business can get your message remembered when it comes time to make a decision. There are many ways to influence the influencers.

Magicians and witches are no strangers to what we call petitioning in the sense of spellcraft. Writing messages on paper and destroying them to manifest an outcome is a standard spell method within many traditions. Applying those principles to the mundane world of petitioning for advocacy is an easy choice.

Writing physical letters provides many options for magical activism:

★ If you are writing the letter by hand rather than typing, try incorporating a magical ink. The juice of pokeberries ensures that things will take root and spread quickly, bearing fruit with ease in the most challenging conditions. There are a number of magical inks available through various occult sellers for different purposes. Make sure you keep your handwriting neat.

★ The paper can be held over your incense censer and blessed before being sent on its way. Choose a blend that corresponds with the feeling you're trying to convey: air blends for sending a message that's clear and relatable, fire blends to express passion and even anger, water blends to play on your target's emotions, and earth blends to show that your commitment to this issue is firm and unwavering.

★ Before dropping your letter in the mailbox or hitting "send" on your email, say a prayer to Hermes, the great messenger god of the ancient Greeks. Hermes can help ensure that your message not only arrives to its destination safely, but is seen, read, and understood. Feel free to make it simple and personal, or word it a bit more formally. Here's my own petition prayer to the great messenger god:

Fleet-footed Hermes, I pray to you.
Beloved of gods and mortals,
Son of Zeus and Maia,
You who stand at all doorways and speed through
    their crossings,
I send this message with your care.

*By your herald's wand let it be received and seen
with haste.
To the Great One with great access, I give praise
and thanks.*

★ Add a small sigil or symbol to the letter to secure power and influence. There are a number of symbols provided in the defense and offense chapters of this book. You can also insert a sacred symbol that relates to the topic of your letter. For example, if you're writing to protect an old oak grove from being demolished, trace the letter Duir (Oak) from the Celtic Ogham alphabet. Keep your symbol small and subtle so it doesn't distract from your letter. You can also add symbols to an email by dropping them in as an image at the top or bottom and then resizing them to make them smaller. If you're filling out a form letter on a website or app, you might not be able to do that. Instead, here's my trick for adding a small and subtle typed spell, inspired by the themes of traditional sigil-making:

Step 1: Come up with your affirmation, incantation, or statement of power. For example:

"As the letter in your hands unfolds, you will save these old oak groves."

Step 2: Take out all vowels and repeating consonant letters:

"s thlr n y d f, w v k g."

Step 3: Close up the spaces and combine the remaining letters in all-caps and place the resulting sigil under your signature:

"Sincerely,
David Salisbury
STHLRNYDFWVKG"

You should feel empowered to get creative and employ your own magical methods for petitioning as a fun and easy way to begin weaving your magic into your activism. Once you're comfortable reaching out to decision-makers at a distance, you might consider the next step: showing up in person.

Lobbying

When most people think of lobbying or lobbyists, they might picture highly paid professionals in Washington hired by large corporations to influence politicians. While that is certainly a major way that lobbying goes on in the United States, that's not what it's all about.

The origins of lobbying span a great deal of time and distance. Some say it originated in the United Kingdom, where members of Parliament would meet with the public in the hallways following debates. Similarly in the United States, it's said to originate with Ulysses S. Grant, who would often get approached in a hotel lobby he frequented in the evening for drinks. Members of the public or other politicians would buy him drinks and ask for special favors. Although that story is fun to think about, *lobbying* as a political term actually appeared in print roughly fifty years before

Grant ever took office, shrouding its true origins in mystery. Wherever it comes from, its impact on politics and activism today cannot be overstated.

Simply put, lobbying is any effort by an individual, organization, or corporation to influence a political body—whether governmental or not—to make decisions that are in the interests of the lobbyist or whomever the lobbyist represents. So while you may think of a lobbyist as a well-paid professional, you can be a lobbyist yourself!

Technically, lobbying is any act of reaching out to a decision-maker personally by any means, whether it's writing, calling, or visiting in person. For our purposes, I'm going to use lobbying to refer to actions that involve in-person visits.

Visiting a decision-maker in person may seem like a big leap of involvement from petitioning, and it is. But if you can find the time and courage to do it, it's an enormously impactful and deeply fulfilling way to make a difference. Lobbying can feel intimidating because we are often conditioned by society to believe that leaders and decision-makers are smarter than we are, unreachable, and uninterested in what we have to say. And while certain people can certainly be unreachable in person (have you tried scheduling a meeting with the secretary of state lately?), there are almost always levels of decision-makers you can gain access to. In the non-political world this can be anyone from a customer service representative to the CEO of a company.

Figuring out the person to meet with in the first place is half the battle. This is where you need to do your research. If you'd like to meet with someone in political office about a piece of legislation, you need to figure out where the bill is and where it will be moving to next. If the bill has already passed your state representative's chamber, then meeting with your state rep isn't going to do much good. But if the next step for the bill is your state senate, then meeting with your state senator is the obvious choice. Finding out who represents you is easily searchable online, and all state representatives and senators have local offices you can get in touch with. If a bill is moving to a committee, then you'll want to get in touch with the members of that committee regardless of whether or not you're their constituent, although you should be aware that some public officials will refuse to meet with anyone who is not a constituent.

With issues of corporate and organizational policy or local municipal politics, things get much easier. Generally, you should try to meet directly with the people who are actually going to influence the issue. In our earlier example of the old oak grove, this might mean meeting with your city council member. Sitting down with a city council member directly isn't usually very challenging, depending on where you live. Your chances of meeting your council member might be slimmer if you live in a place like New York City where the city council is almost as prominent and in-demand as the Senate; your chances are better if you live in a smaller city or town.

In the case of our oak grove, you would want to get in touch with the council member's office in advance and see if they even have any sway at all. They might tell you that the situation is already out of their hands and in the domain of a corporation. In that case, you can still pressure them to use their voice to influence whoever can make that change. Companies know that they need to stay in the good graces of local governments who can decide things like zoning and tax breaks for companies and their employees.

With your lobbying target determined, it's time to set up the meeting. If you're meeting with public officials at a level higher than your city or county government, be prepared for meeting with the official's staff rather than that official personally. Although this is obviously less than ideal, it is normal. Don't worry, the time an office spends on having staff meet with constituents is recorded and noted for the official and considerably impactful in most cases. The meeting will almost always be held on a weekday between 9 a.m. and 5 p.m., so be aware of that in case you need to take some time off work. You won't need much. Lobbying meetings are typically quite short. There are many people who even make time for them on their lunch breaks if their office is close enough!

Be sure that you're on time for your meeting, ideally showing up early just in case. Remember to dress well, keeping in mind the advice of "focusing on the message rather than the messenger." When you meet with the decision-maker or their staff, you should have some talking points prepared that get directly to the facts, why the issue is important to you, and what you need them to do about it. If the office has already taken a stance on the issue, they may interject and explain their reasoning. This can be off-putting if their position is against yours. Do not let that deter you or make you lose focus. Decision-makers can always change their mind, especially with input from constituents and customers. Here are some short tips for making sure the conversation goes your way:

★ Avoid being too argumentative, but do stand firm and confident with your position. State each point and move on rather than getting into a circular debate that reiterates the same point, which can be a waste of time. Although it can be intimidating to lobby at first, remember that these people work for you (if meeting with politicians) or you're the one potentially paying their salaries (if meeting with a company or organization).

★ If the person you're speaking with challenges you by bringing up a point you're not familiar with, you can choose to not acknowledge it and simply return to your talking point. This is a very basic part of discussion and debate that both politicians and the media are familiar with. For example:

Staffer: *But Mr. Salisbury, there is evidence that the oaks could be in danger of a disease that's sweeping through this part of the state and that they'll die off eventually. That's why we want to cut to the chase and get rid of them now.*

Me: *I'm not familiar with this disease, but what I do know is that this grove is a cherished part of our local community. I'm interested in the current state of the oaks, which is a place where children have played and animals have made their homes in for decades.*

This tactic can take some practice, but it's a wonderful debate tool if you can master it. Practice with a friend in advance of your meeting and have them challenge you with similar statements and see how you respond. Record yourself with a video and play it back to see how confident you appear and to figure out what you might need to work on.

★ Always bring the conversation to a close by restating exactly what you'd like to see happen, followed by thanking the person or people for their time. If they've made some kind of commitment to you in the meeting, ask for a time frame or a way to follow up on when it will be accomplished.

After lobbying I like to write a short thank-you card. Aside from being polite, it helps the office remember the person they spoke with and reinforces your commitment to seeing this issue through. A post-meeting thank-you card might go something like this:

Dear Council Member,

Thank you for meeting with me last Thursday morning. It was a pleasure to meet with your staff and discuss the importance of our cherished community oak grove.

As we discussed, the animal habitats for the grove in addition to the natural play setting for kids that the grove provides are an invaluable resource for our community. I look forward to seeing the next steps to ensure that we do whatever we can to preserve the land. I've included my contact information on the back of this card if you'd like to follow up with me again.

Sincerely,
David Salisbury
STHLRNYDFWVKG

You can also include any of the magical tips for petitioning in your lobbying follow-up letter, as I've done above with our signature spell.

When incorporating magic with physical meetings, you'll need to be subtler and more creative. The staff might look at you rather suspiciously if you barge in brandishing a wand and saying an incantation—they might even call security if they don't have a sense of humor. Many of my magical techniques for lobbying involve using it before and after a meeting, and maybe a little during.

Before the meeting. Focus on yourself first. Work magic that improves your confidence and communication skills. Give offerings to Hermes, asking for his aid in becoming an effective messenger. Do the same with Athena, a goddess of political expertise and war negotiations that benefit communities. Consider putting a stone in your pocket ahead of time. It is thought that carrying agate will make the wearer more persuasive around others, for example.

During the meeting. This is where you'll have to be a bit subtler. One of my favorite tricks is to trace a small sigil of influence and persuasion on the inside of my dominant hand in washable marker. When you get to the meeting and shake hands, the power of the sigil will "rub off" on them. If you're in an office and waiting to be met, focus on the boundaries of your personal aura and imagine it stretching farther and farther out until it encases the whole room. Not only will that make you feel more confident and powerful for the meeting, but it makes those within your personal bubble more prone to your influence.

After the meeting. This is where you have a lot of room to use a variety of magical techniques to push things in favor of your issue. You might like to craft a custom spell designed around how your meeting went. If the person says that they don't have the resources to accomplish what you need, then you might do a working to send prosperity and connections to aid your goal. If they seem entirely resistant to the issue for their own reasons, then you might decide to get more aggressive and work magic focused on pushing them aside so that favorable influences can gain the upper hand. You'll learn more about this in the Building an Offense chapter.

I've had some excellent lobbying experiences and some truly awful ones. Some visits leave you feeling like you've truly made a huge impact for the better while others might leave you feeling pretty hopeless about the way this world is run. No matter what your experiences are, know that you'll be among a very small number of people who ever take the time and effort to attempt to have these types of conversations face-to-face. I truly believe that above all, genuine human interaction is the biggest change-maker of all.

Outreach and Volunteering

Outreach is a way of connecting with your peers or your community around you about an issue rather than appealing directly to a decision-maker. Consider it a type of recruitment designed to bring others on board with your issue. If you've ever been handed a leaflet on the street, asked to sign a petition, or had a video shared with you about an issue, you've experienced outreach. Outreach can feel uncomfortable for some magic workers in Pagan communities which discourage proselytizing and efforts to convert others. But it's important to make a distinction here: religious conversion is very different from letting others know about something verifiably wrong in the world and empowering them with the information to change it.

Telling others about an issue is only the first part of the process; on its own I'd call it education, as discussed earlier. Outreach goes to the next step by incorporating an ask. It's one thing to tell your neighbors that the cherished oak grove is scheduled to be destroyed. It's another to add the ask to visit a town hall meeting about it. Or you might ask them to boycott the company responsible. Outreach is meant to cause a ripple effect and get others involved in being the change.

The basics of outreach are generally simple, but it comes with its own share of complexities. On the simple side, all you really need to do is make sure you have an ask associated with the information you're giving out. Even if the ask is simply to spread the word if there is no actionable item to tell someone about just yet, make sure to include that. This is also important because people tend to shut down when they hear bad news that they can't do anything about. Make it as easy as possible for people to take action. Bring the resources to take action as close to them as possible.

The tricky part of outreach is usually the approach. New activists can get overexcited by the thrill of making a difference in the world and can come off as overbearing. Remember that no one likes being lectured to or told what to do. While there are certainly things that we should strongly decry and be angry about, I find it most effective to talk to peers on an even footing, where you're both approaching the subject as equal citizens. Be aware that however kindly you reach out to someone, there will always be people who consider any form of outreach an overstep. Some people don't want to know, don't care, and won't act. As unfortunate as that is, you just have to reclaim your time and move on quickly to someone else who will. Outreach isn't about proving that you're persuasive enough to bring someone on board. Remember to keep your focus on the issue and you'll eventually win.

Volunteering is obviously a more direct approach that gets right into the heart of the issue itself. So instead of lobbying your city council on increased care for citizens experiencing homelessness, you'd be showing up to a shelter for food prep and dish duty. Instead of leafleting at a marketplace about the horrid conditions pigs face on factory farms, you'd be spreading hay around a farmed animal sanctuary on your day off.

Incorporating direct volunteering into your activism is important for a number of reasons. For starters, it allows you to see the situation firsthand rather than reading about it or watching a documentary. That helps you tell the stories of your issue with a greater sense of authenticity. Second, it can feel incredibly fulfilling to immediately see how your efforts are helping to make things better. While we should certainly be careful about not making ourselves the focus of the work, being fulfilled in the work helps to prevent burnout and ensures that you'll keep coming back to help.

If you've never volunteered before—or have for a specific cause but not another—be aware that it is not always what you think it's going to be. It's important to accept that and show up for whatever work is most needed.

When I was twenty-two, I signed up to volunteer a few times a week at a local soup kitchen in Washington, D.C. I had imagined I'd be right in the serving line meeting guests, hearing their stories, and getting to connect with people one-on-one. That's what I wanted and expected, and I figured I'd be great at it. I love meeting new people. Instead, I got put in the back washing out huge cooking pots all morning with no access to anyone. I was irritated at first until I realized that the kitchen was in deep need of someone to do this particular work. The cooks were doing double the work by washing dishes and preparing the meals at the same time, putting the whole operation under strain. My contribution was important whether I noticed it or not. I'm sad to admit that for a time, I had made the work about me. It was a lesson in humility that I consider invaluable to this day. Here's my best advice about volunteering: if you're asked to be a soup pot scrubber at 5 a.m., be the best damn soup pot scrubber that place has ever seen. It matters.

When working magic into outreach and volunteering, it's all about doing spells that focus on improving your own self. Working directly with the beings and places that are the center of your issue is best done when you're operating within your true authentic self. I've mentioned authenticity several times already because being connected with your true nature is vital for creating experiences that take root.

Magical traditions all over the world have countless exercises designed to align the various parts of the self in a way that helps one remain connected, clean, and whole. In my own personal practice, I do this through a tool from the Anderson Feri tradition of witchcraft. Soul alignment is a way to get the different parts of us speaking so that a greater channel of power can flow cleanly through us. It is recommended within Feri that soul alignment be performed every day, and I certainly endorse this as well. For our purposes, it is particularly useful with outreach, volunteering, or any act that requires you to engage in direct acts of compassion.

Soul Alignment

The concept of soul alignment is based on a three-soul cosmology. It is built on the idea that we are made up of various soul parts playing various roles in our existence. Each soul part is equally valuable, and the goal of soul alignment is to bring all three into conversation with one another. Think of it like a computer switchboard, where all portions of the program must be connected for optimal success. When our souls are aligned, we have greater access to our power, our divine nature, our base instincts, and our deep mind.

The three soul parts are as follows:

1. **Fetch.** Located around the sex regions of the body and also thought to cover the body in a thin layer right on top of the skin. Also called the Lower Self, fetch is responsible for instinct, survival, desire, hunger, ego, vitality, and all things related to the body and one's "gut instinct." Fetch can communicate directly with our Godsoul.

2. **Talker.** Located around the torso and thought to circle the body as a sphere (the aura). Talker is our outward conscious body responsible for processing our thoughts and communicating them to the outside world. Talker tries to make sense of things, whether

that is helpful or not. Talker is all about the personality and thrives when individuality and personal ideas are expressed. Talker can only communicate directly with Fetch.

3. **Godsoul.** Located about six inches above the head or around the head as a halo or sphere. Also called the Holy Dove or Higher Self. Godsoul is our pure, perfect nature. It is everything about us that stretches toward divinity and holiness. Godsoul is responsible for our eternal connection to infinity and all contained within it. Godsoul cannot typically communicate directly to Talker and requires Fetch as a sort of translator.

Begin by breathing slowly and deeply, allowing yourself to relax, muscle by muscle. As you get comfortable with the exercise, you may wish to dim the lights or even play some relaxing music. The breath is the most important thing here. You should patiently allow your breath to take you down into a relaxed and centered state.

Focus your attention on Fetch. Continuing to breathe, allow feelings of survival, instinct, and desire to well up within you. What is Fetch telling you? What does it need? What does it have to offer? On your exhale, feel the energy of Fetch expanding within and around you.

Raise your attention up to Talker. Continuing to breathe, allow feelings of personal expression, worldly success and failure, and your current place in the world to well up within you. What is Talker telling you? What does it need? What does it have to offer? On your exhale, feel the energy of Talker expanding within and around you.

Allow your attention to rise high up into Godsoul. Continuing to breathe, allow the knowledge of your divine perfection to well up within you. You are a strong, whole, and eternal being. Know this and own it. What is Godsoul telling you? What does it need? What does it have to offer? On your exhale, feel the energy of Godsoul expanding within and around you.

Rapidly return your attention to Fetch, and with a sharp inhale, pull in energy to Fetch and store it there. With another sharp inhale, shoot it up to Talker and let it rest there. With another sharp inhale, push that energy back down to Fetch.

Now, with your biggest inhale, pull in all your power to Fetch. On your next exhale, tilt your head upward and sharply exhale the breath as you vocalize—preferably shouting—the sound "HA!"

Feel the energy and breath rush up from Fetch and hit Godsoul like a firework. It explodes into an ecstatic burst of power and umbrellas like a fountain above your head.

The energy then cascades down around you, like a shining waterfall, blessing the other soul parts in its descent, until it rests at last with Fetch.

Repeat aloud, even if in a whisper:

> *All three souls are aligned within me.*
> *All three souls are aligned within me.*
> *All three souls are aligned within me.*
> *So mote it be.*

Breathe comfortably as you feel your souls aligned as one. If you received any insights or sensations from any of your souls, now would be a great time to record them.

....

Street Activism:
Marching and Demonstrating

Street activism is what automatically comes to mind for many people when they hear the word *activism*. The whole production of putting on demonstrations and marching through the street is a time-honored visual of the classic activist. As we've already explored, there is so much more to activism than taking the fight to the streets, but being in the streets and putting yourself on display is a down tactic for a very good reason: attention.

Human beings have very short attention spans—particularly today when everyone is struggling to be seen and heard amid an unprecedented volume of media confronting us nearly all day, every day. In addition to our other work that may seem more low-key, there are times when it becomes necessary to demand that we be seen and heard. Marching and demonstrating serve a variety of purposes all at once: gaining media attention for an issue, vocally showing solidarity with others and lifting our collective morale, pressuring decision-makers in public, and generally raising the overall profile of an issue.

Because of the high visibility of street activism, it can be one of the first ways that someone ever gets involved with justice work. When I was eleven years old, my father, who was a union worker at the time, brought me along to a union march one summer focused on demanding higher wages and better working conditions. I was fascinated with the whole spectacle of it all: the giant blow-up props, the colorful signs, the megaphones, the linked arms. . . . I remember having a strong sense that I wanted to do things like that someday. A few years later in my freshman year in high school with those thoughts still fresh in my head, I started getting involved with local protests for animal rights and LGBTQ students. Clearly the public appeal of demonstrating had a moving effect that carried me into the work I do today. That's the ripple effect we're looking for.

While lobbying and petitioning usually follow a set formula, street activism can look wildly different from event to event. I've been to demonstrations with as few as three people standing on the street and holding up a small banner to massive events like the Women's March on Washington in 2017, which held anywhere from half a million to a million demonstrators.

Demonstration is most often a broad term, but I like to limit it to actions that are focused on displaying a message through some kind of artistic means. That can mean displaying banners and signs, performing street theater, or having any kind of intentful visual display. Demonstrations (or demos) don't require many people to be effective since the people involved are simply facilitating the delivery of a message. Whether it's projecting a message in light on a building at night or dressing up in costumes on a street corner, demonstrations use the power of creativity to send a message that grabs attention and helps your onlookers remember it.

Marching can be considered a type of demonstration, but the success of such events is traditionally tied to the number of marchers rather than what they're carrying or displaying. Personally, I think there are a great many other factors beyond size that can make or break a march, but it is undeniable that marches with impressive numbers leave lasting impressions. Marches are far more challenging to organize than simple street demonstrations and usually require permits to be filed, planned meetings with local officials, and other logistical items that can make setting them up a real challenge without strong people power and funding.

Street activism of all types comes with a certain level of risk. While you're not likely to be harassed or harmed while lobbying an official or making a phone call, chances significantly increase once you put your body out into a public space. The risks can vary greatly from being harassed by police who don't know what your protest rights are—or simply don't care—to challenges by counterprotesters and angry onlookers to the demonstration itself going sour and breaking out into riots—whether instigated by the demonstrators themselves or by police, both of which are equally likely. That said, street activism is something that's been a major part of my life since my teenage years, and it's exceedingly rare that I've ever felt at risk. Of course, I have an enormous amount of societal privilege that protects me in these situations. Your mileage will vary, which is why I've included instructions on personal protection at physical street activism events in the Building a Defense chapter of this book.

All magical methods from lobbying and other in-person events apply while engaging in a demonstration or march. Place a strong focus on drawing attention to your message and having it be widely seen by the people around you.

Civil Disobedience and Direct Action

We cannot do justice to discussions of activism without including civil disobedience and direct action. The United States in particular has a proud history of citizens who did their activist work outside the bounds of the law, bringing forth a better society because of it. From the Boston Tea Party of the American Revolution to the lunch counter protests of the civil rights movement and many others, purposefully breaking the law is woven into the fabric of political and social change.

Civil disobedience is generally defined as any type of activism that breaks the law to any varying degree. It can be as small as standing on a sidewalk designated as "private" for a demonstration or as large as disrupting an event or even causing damage to property. Direct action is a type of civil disobedience, although it may or may not be illegal. For example, a same-sex couple demanding a marriage license in an area where marriage equality is not yet the reality could be considered a gentle type of direct action. It is not my place to endorse, condemn, or condone civil disobedience or the avoidance of it. Instead, I'd like us to think about how communities that have had little to no other recourse for justice have been forced to make their voices heard. As with all activism, we must practice empathy by putting ourselves in the shoes of others to the greatest possible extent.

The greatest debates about civil disobedience tend to focus on how effective or detrimental it is to a movement. In my experience, activists with a strong knowledge of social history tend to agree that lawbreaking has been monumentally effective in the past and continues to be so today. Others argue that certain types of civil disobedience give "bad press" and push movements out of favor with the general public. Whatever your stance comes to be, it's important to remember that we all have different reasons for using the methods we do to create change.

Magic for Change

Now that we've looked at various types of activism, we need to explore how to apply magic to those actions. How do these two fields of endeavor overlap, and where can magic have an impact? We can approach activism with the same mind-set as a magical problem and double our effectiveness by adding magical approaches to mundane ones.

Establishing Intent

In the many ways that activism and magic intersect, there is perhaps no better example than the establishment of intent. In the most basic sense, establishing an intent means forming a clear and direct statement of what you desire and how you plan on obtaining that desire.

In the Western traditions of magic there is a saying that many modern magic workers have come to call "The Witch's Pyramid," or Four Powers of the Sphinx. The base of the pyramid has four points: to know, to will, to dare, and to keep silent. Some may assign "to go" to the peak of the pyramid. The pyramid reminds us of the fundamental keys to performing effective magic.

Knowing is the core of what we need to establish intent. With knowledge of a situation and what we intend to do about it, we can then move forward with a solid base. When we engage our Will, we align our power, skill, and knowledge to charge up the intention. When we Dare, we set these various pieces in motion through the courage and tenacity it takes to fuse our intentions with our will. In Keeping Silent, we employ the wisdom of understanding when to pick up our goal and run with it and when to allow it to settle and gestate until it's ready to sprout.

With the Witch's Pyramid in mind, here's a questionnaire you can use to establish intent and clearly define your goal:

1. What are the many details of the situation and how would you like it to change? Be as specific as possible.

2. Based on your answer to the first question, boil your statement down and phrase it as a single sentence.

3. What are some things you will do in the physical world and magically to change the situation?

4. What will your indicators of success be? List anything that would show progress toward the goal along with what things will look like once the goal has completely manifested.

As you start to roll out your plan, be aware that your intention might change along the way. Advocacy campaigns both simple and complex can involve shifting dynamics that might alter your course. Your goal could end up as a negotiating point between different sides of the issue or begin to lose the support it may have enjoyed. Or the communities directly affected by the issue could come out and state they'd like something entirely different done with the situation. The clever activist knows how to adapt the game plan with changing dynamics. The clever witch knows how to shift their magical intent to accommodate a shifting environment.

Applying a Method

With our intent established we can incorporate the pyramid's points of Will and Daring to set things in motion. It's time to talk about how we plan to actually create this change. What are the methods both physically and spiritually we can use to best achieve our goals?

When it comes to magic, we have centuries' worth of systems, teaching, and techniques to draw from. If you're already part of an established magical tradition, whether as a student or an initiate, it may be easy to pick from the options available to you. If you tend to be a more eclectic worker or just like to experiment with a number of magical methods, you might like to spend more time considering the type of magic you'd like to use for your goal. In general I like to think that the type of magic we use doesn't matter as much as the wisdom and skill we apply when working it. That said, there are some things I like to keep in mind when deciding what type of working I want to do.

The first thing to consider is your timeline. Is your campaign or goal something you know will take a very long time to accomplish or is this something that you might be able to wrap up in just a few days? Magical workings toward getting fair-trade chocolate added to your local co-op could be very different from magic worked for removing a bigoted politician who has three years left in office. In general, short-term goals need fewer and less complex workings while long-term goals might require the same working to repeat over time with more thought and energy put into things. Here's a quick list I refer to when determining the type of working I'll use based on the breadth of the situation:

Immediate Goal (0–30 days): Prayer work, creative visualization, chanting and mantras, sigils

Short-Term Goal (1–6 months): Small candle spells, charm crafting, onetime rituals

Extended Goal (6 months–1 year): Multiple rituals, spirit servitors, seven-day candle spells

Long-Term Goal (multiyear): All of the above methods applied from early in the campaign to later

In theory, you could apply any of the above methods at any stage of a campaign. The timeline I've used is based on how much effort is typically required with these types of workings combined with how long each type of magic takes to manifest along with how long each type tends to last.

Prayer Work. Praying to various entities may or may not even be considered magic by some. Prayers are easy to employ, take little effort, and tend to ask for low amounts of energy, which make them ideal for short-term goals. Send your prayers to beings who tend to be more amicable to your type of goal or those with whom you have a special relationship.

Creative Visualization. Considered to be a staple of most spells, creative visualization can also be used on its own to gently influence the energetics of a situation. The most basic form of visualization involves calming your mind, closing your eyes, and clearly imagining what you'd like to happen. Some people struggle with visualization as a skill, while others find it quite easy. If you don't already consider yourself adept at even basic visualization, I highly recommend some regular practice.

Chanting and Mantras. Many magicians agree we manifest what we breathe and speak aloud. Breath is life, and the sounds we produce create vibrations that get sent out into the world for manifestation, whether we mean them to or not. A mantra is typically a phrase, short prayer, or set of sacred words repeated over and over to generate energy and manifest a goal. In modern magic, they are usually spoken as if the goal has already occurred. For example, a local activist running for a seat on the city council might say "The city council seat is mine" rather than "I hope I win this city council seat." Stating something as if it is already the current reality creates a vibrational pattern that sets up an easy manifestation. When creating a chant, it's important that you keep it short and directly to the point. This will allow you to speak it quickly while keeping your Will clearly defined.

Sigils. I discuss sigils regularly in this book, as they are some of my favorite magical tools. A sigil is any type of symbol or script that carries a magical significance. They can be personal to the magician or tried-and-true symbols employed by a tradition or culture for a long time. Sigils are great for immediate goals because they carry latent power that doesn't require a lot of constant energy to make them useful. Tracing a sigil onto a situation, whether physically or energetically, is a fast and easy way to shift the vibrational energy of the environment.

Candle Spells. Candles are wonderful tools for short-term goals because they're easy to set up and can pack quite a punch. In spellcraft, the candle anchors the goal with a physical focal point as a storage unit or funnel to communicate the desired goal. This makes candles highly adaptable tools that can be put to use quickly and repeatedly (if needed) over the course of several weeks or months.

Charms. *Charm* is a very broad term, but I use it to designate a type of physical talisman or amulet meant to pull something in or repel something, respectively. A charm can be anything from a necklace with a sacred stone or sigil, a cotton bag with herbs and roots stored within it, a spell written on a piece of paper and bound up in twine, or any other small and portable item you can place in a specific location or carry on your person. I love using charms for short-term goals because I can carry them with me in a great number of situations and go back and recharge them if my goal ends up taking longer to manifest than I initially anticipated.

Rituals. Obviously, rituals can vary in scale from something that can take three minutes or several hours to perform. I consider a ritual to be something that involves assembling multiple components. For a spell, a ritual might add in the invocation of deities or spirits for assistance, the creation of a sacred space to ground the power, and multiple forms of magic. For short-term goals, it may be wise to consider doing a ritual at the beginning of a campaign to begin to apply multiple sources of power. Rituals can be adapted, changed, and repeated as the dynamics of a situation change.

Spirit Servitors. A spirit servitor is a being either created by the magician or summoned for a specific task and only that task. After the task is completed, the spirit is dismissed or, in the case of a spirit the magician has created themselves, destroyed. Sending forth a spirit to aid in the accomplishment of a goal is perfect for long-term plans. As intelligent beings, spirits can take care of things when we're not able to pay attention to something ourselves—no one has the ability to keep an eye on their goal 24/7—and help influence matters directly even when the magician is far away from the focal point.

Seven-Day Candle Spells. Seven-day candles are a popular tool within the field of candle magic and are typically used for goals that might take some time to manifest. In form, they're the traditional Catholic prayer candles you see in churches or in Catholic supply shops. As the name indicates, they are usually charged once and then lit every day for seven days. They can also be lit once a week for several weeks, and so on, depending on the estimated amount of time the goal might take to manifest. I love using seven-day candle spells for long-term goals because once the initial effort is put in, it's quite easy to keep the magic going with a simple flick of my lighter.

Aside from the length of time, it is helpful to consider the type of action you need to do. For engaging in a multiweek letter-writing campaign, a seven-day candle spell would be useful, lighting up your charged candle each time you begin to put pen to paper or your fingers on the keyboard. At times when an action comes up suddenly, like an emergency demonstration, you may need to use magic that can stay portable, such as sigils, creative visualization, or carrying a charm with you. Once again we have an opportunity to get creative and clever. Let's take a look at a sample scenario and how I might approach it.

Sample Scenario: An Elephant Tragedy

The local zoo in my city has an abhorrent history of cruelty to the animals it holds captive. Not only does it hire staff who neglect the animals with improper care, but the small and artificial conditions in this particular zoo deprive the animals of everything natural to them, with larger animals suffering in particular. Although local citizens have known about this for a while, we then heard about an especially painful tragedy. A recently born baby elephant at the zoo, named Lana, ate some trash left in her enclosure and died of it.

Activists in our local community were ready to spring into action. But what could we do? We know that in the long term, the city council would be considering legislation with demands for greater care and better habitats for any captive endangered animal within the city limits. While we could continue to push for that to pass, we knew that it would be another six months at least before the council could consider it. In the meantime, our local activists agreed that we could use the event to draw attention to the plight of captive elephants in general. Additionally, we decided to call upon the zoo to immediately evaluate all staff procedures regarding the care of enclosures and demand that this particular staffer not be allowed to work with animals again.

We determined that while the tragedy was still in the news, we'd conduct a basic sign-holding demonstration in front of the zoo within a couple days and invite the media to cover it. That would draw attention to the issue in general. Then, we'd start a call-in campaign over the next couple of weeks targeting the zoo's director to make the enclosure changes and remove the staffer from the direct handling of the animals.

With our physical actions in place, it was time to apply our magic. For our demonstration, I wanted to focus on drawing as much attention from the media and public as possible. For that, I made a glamour sigil, designed to draw eyes toward what we were doing. I crafted the sigil using a basic single eye drawing with the name "LANA" written underneath it in a magical alphabet. To add some strength to the sigil, I empowered it by writing a short chant that I repeatedly breathed into it: "Let all see what has been done unto this creature till we've won." While chanting, I painted the sigil onto the back of the signs we'd created for the demonstration. I also wrote it extremely small on the back of the information flyers printed for the media and pass-ersby at the demonstration.

For our more serious goal of getting the zoo to adopt changes to enclosures and launch a detailed investigation, I wrote a basic candle spell focused on justice. I took a blue pillar candle and started by inscribing my sigil into it. Next, I anointed it with olive oil sacred to Athena, a goddess of policy change, and rolled it in powdered chili pepper because I want to add the spicy aspects of the fire elements to bring justice, manifestation, or change as quickly as possible. I lit the candle every night, each time speaking the chant I'd written.

While all of that was happening, I decided to also lend magical assistance to the legislation up before the city council. During the six months before the bill will be con-sidered, I will add my sigil to the letters that my friends and I write to our council members. If we manage to get a meeting with council members, we'll speak the chant I've written while waiting in the lobby and practice visualiza-tion, imagining ourselves shaking hands with an agreeable council member in celebration of their commitment to act on our behalf.

If obstacles pop up during this time, I might also incor-porate other methods such as using banishing spells to clear away obstacles and keep the path to success open.

There are many ways that I could have approached this scenario. It can be tempting to overthink things and fret about the "right way" to apply a method. I generally like to keep things simple and build from there. Once you start slowly incorporating magical methods into your work, the right thing to do will start to come naturally to you. As long as your will is established and you know what you'd like to happen, you've embarked upon a path to success.

Raising Power

Now that we're familiar with some of the "tech" of our common magical methods, we need to become comfortable with the various ways we can raise power for those methods. While designing a sigil or writing a chant can be effective in its own right, it is always worth it to add power to whatever we're working. On the Witch's Pyramid, this is what some modern magicians might consider the apex of To Go: we need to give our magical vehicles the gasoline they need to hit the road.

Magic workers have a seemingly infinite number of options when it comes to raising energy. Entire books have been written on the topic, and I've attended workshops about this subject that have lasted four full days. While it is certainly worth it to become well versed in a number of power-raising methods, we can keep it simple for now, applying techniques that are easy to master with just a little practice.

Breath

Breath is considered one of the most basic yet important methods of raising power. If you cannot control the breath, it is going to be very challenging to perform effective magic. Breath is life, and the powers we conjure rely on the breath, whether directly or indirectly. When we breathe into or through something, we are giving that thing life. Outside of formal spellwork, breath also allows us to control the status of our own bodies, granting us the ability to either enter into a deep calm or hype ourselves up for an intense activity when needed.

There are many techniques for breath work, but at the very least we should understand how to use it to raise power within the body quickly and then direct it toward our goal.

For a basic energy raising, consider a common technique I call the "two by two" breath. First, allow yourself to become conscious of your normal flow of breath, noticing every inhale and exhale. When you're ready to raise the power, take two sharp and fast breaths in, then exhale two sharp and fast breaths out. You can do this slowly at first and then increase the pace as you go. This might feel rather dizzying at first, especially if it's your first time. Do this until you feel that you cannot continue it any longer. In your final two sharp inhales, store the breath for a few seconds deep into your solar plexus and then with one breath quickly exhale all at once. When you exhale, you should ideally point your breath toward any physical focal point of the spell, like a candle, charm, sigil, etc. If you don't have a physical focal point, tilt your head up to the sky and project the breath upward while affirming your intent.

For raising power intended to help you become grounded and centered, you'll want to keep the breath slow and drawn out. A common method is a ten-second cyclical breath. Breathe in for the count of ten, hold that breath for the count of ten, exhale on the count of ten, hold that exhale for another ten, and then repeat. This slows down the heart rate and will cause you to rapidly settle into the body. If you have a medical condition that causes labored breathing, you may want to cut this down to five-second counts or check with your physician.

Movement

Moving our bodies is what most magic workers immediately think of when we discuss raising power. In movement, we can really feel the power being generated in our bodies. Our heart rate increases, our blood quickens, we get warm and maybe even feel a type of high if the movement is fast and sustained enough. (Folks who run for exercise will be familiar with this.) Movement can also be easily adapted to just about any situation, space conditions, or number of people.

Basic power movements can be done by yourself just with your hands. Press your palms together, lightly at first, and rub them against each other. Increase the pace and pressure slowly as you go, rubbing faster and harder. You'll feel your arms getting tired and your hands getting hot. When you feel like you can't keep it up anymore, stop all at once and project your hands out to your focal point. You'll notice how the blood flow and friction on the skin causes the hands to become tingly and sensitive.

You can also utilize your whole body through a number of methods including rocking, swaying, dancing, running (typically around in a circle), and twirling. Different magical traditions can turn to specific methods for specific purposes.

Voice

Singing, chanting, and intoning sounds enjoy a rich depth of spiritual lore from around the world. Transcending religion and stretching across countless cultures, using our voice to summon powers and raise our own is a tradition nearly as old as civilization itself. Although some would consider voice methods as falling under the category of breath, I consider them two separate things, as the type of power raised tends to feel so different. When we sing or chant, we're tapping into vibrational energy or the energies adrift in the space around us. By tapping into that energy, we align it with our own and come into connection and conversation with the land and—when singing together—with our communities. Many of us have felt how amazing it is to be at a wonderful concert with everyone around singing in unison with the performer. This same kind of energizing experience is also found in some of the Christian denominations of the South which, despite the social justice issues some of them have, are really onto something with the use of big choruses for praise and worship.

Singing is a strong part of many justice movements throughout history. We can look to the fight for freedom for African Americans of the United States for a moving example. "Follow the Drinking Gourd" was used as a type of "song map" (the "drinking gourd" being the Milky Way) to assist slaves in the South in finding the pathways to freedom in the North. It continued to resonate through the civil rights movements of the 1950s and '60s.

Songs and chants, aside from being inspirational, can act as instructions and even spells. In many forms of Western Ceremonial Magic, magical words are intoned or deeply vibrated in the throat to direct power and instruct the spirit forces on what needs to be done. The activism-focused Reclaiming Tradition of witchcraft is particularly good at this, employing songs and chants as instructional spells in marches, protests, and rallies.

Follow-Through

After applying our strategic method of action and raising power toward our goals, the final consideration is to plan for follow-through. Simply put, what will you do after the spell has been cast, the charm crafted, or the ritual enacted? Even if you've worked magic after your main action, it is helpful to be mindful of how your campaign is doing and to continue to apply pressure. This is true in the magical sense as well as the material one. Here are two checklists you can use to keep your follow-through plans solid and moving.

Material Follow-Through

* Communicate. Write follow-up letters and make phone calls to check in about the progress of your goal.

* Stay in touch with your comrades and allies about how things are going. Keep them involved with the follow-through process. If you're not in a leadership role in the campaign, get in touch with the organizers and ask if there's anything you can do to stay involved.

* Keep the publicity drumbeat going. It's easy for a campaign to lose steam once the main action is complete. Keep promoting the cause on social media, speaking out about it with friends, and advertising it however you can.

* Begin to look ahead at your next steps. If you're an organizer, you should have the next phases of your campaign charted out based on the various potential

scenarios for how things could turn out. If you're a participant, be aware that you might soon be called upon to help with the next set of actions.

Magical Follow-Through

★ Keep an altar focused on your goal and lend it regular energy by lighting candles, praying to activist ancestors, and charging your campaign materials on its surface.

★ Keep your protective efforts up. Refer to the chapter on "Building a Defense" for details. Sometimes there can be negative backlash by the opposition during a campaign.

★ Continue working spells designed to push decision-makers into action if things are slow. Consider incorporating the powers of the element of fire to "heat things up" and to keep everything moving along.

★ Look to staying self-aligned, grounded, and energized. Don't be afraid to focus magic on keeping yourself refreshed and empowered. It's very important to avoid activist burnout.

With an understanding of the basic needs of the magical activism and the methods we might use to manifest our goals, we're ready to hit the streets—and the altars!—and create some change. The next step will be strategizing for specific campaigns and preparing ourselves for potential opportunities, pitfalls, and curveballs that might come our way.

Getting to Work

Strategizing

Having some kind of strategy or knowing the strategies at work in a campaign is a crucial element to being effective as activists and magicians. It's not enough to develop the knowledge and resources of what we can do. We need to understand why we plan to do something, learn about the people and forces involved—both allied with us and opposing us—and establish how to communicate what we're doing to the world and how to build and maintain lasting relationships with the communities involved.

Folks new to either activism or magic might feel tempted to always go into a situation "guns blazing," so to speak. We feel passionate and empowered to make change, so we throw everything we have at a situation, hoping that something sticks. I know I'm not alone in having been that person in the past. It is admirable to want to give our whole selves to the work of creating meaningful change. However, a weapon that is poorly aimed isn't good for anyone, including the one who wields it. Developing a strategy—or following one that's already been laid out for us—allows us to use our powers wisely and efficiently, with the maximum potential for success.

Strategizing can have its own shadow side. Sometimes an activist might spend too much time mulling over strategy and not enough time engaged with the actual work. This can certainly be the case when you have many people, groups, and organizations working toward a common goal. No one is ever going to agree on the best way to formulate a plan of action. While it's always good to try and bring people together, attempting to maintain absolute consensus about a strategy at all times can drag a campaign down and cause it to lose steam. Consider your strategy as part of the larger picture of your work, but don't let overanalyzing prevent you from taking those first steps into action.

Gathering Intelligence

Aside from knowing the ins and outs of our issues and causes to the best of our ability, it is also crucial that we gather intelligence about the forces at work in a campaign before we take action.

I like to look first at the people involved who may support my goal or oppose it. In gathering intel about my potential supporters, I can begin to build a base of people who can be mobilized to take action. Think about this both on the grassroots level—talking to regular citizens, family, friends, and colleagues—and on a larger scale with leaders—government officials, corporate allies, vocal community members, and other influencers.

Potential allies could include anyone who's previously acted in support of this type of issue before, folks directly affected by the issue, or anyone who might have interests adjacent to your cause (for example, pro-choice activists tend to also support LGBTQ issues and vice versa). Relating different causes to each other and pointing out why it's important to look at all of them is called *intersectionality*. Intersectionality brings communities together by placing a focus on our commonalities instead of our differences. When activists for different causes are united, our voices become louder and our strengths become stronger. Intersectionality also cultivates empathy within an individual activist: once we look outside of ourselves to the things that are important to others, we're in better positions to engage across the board with a variety of communities. Intersectionality can keep us from falling into the trap of not listening to the communities we are claiming to help. Developing intersectionality will give your cause and mission a larger pool of intelligence, wisdom, and resources to draw from. In return, activists for other causes can draw from your strengths too. This is a great example of the magical concept of "power with" rather than "power over."

The next stage of gathering intelligence about people is looking at those who might oppose your cause. This is important because surprise opposition can disrupt the flow of your campaign. While your mission may focus on a specific person or key set of people who opposed your mission, other less visible opponents can potentially throw a wrench in your work.

In gathering intelligence about your opposition, the first step is to understand the organizational structure—if any— that your opposition has already established. If your work will be focused on opposing the policies of the current administration of the White House, for example, you'd want to not only understand who the main leaders in the administration are, such as the president and vice president, but also the cabinet members, deputies, and other thinkers and strategists who are fueling the work. If your issue is based on a smaller community level, then you'd want to investigate not only the goals and ideals of those opposition community members, but also any political allies they might have. In that case, you might be looking at city council members, local community activists, or public figures like radio talk show hosts or local celebrities. Understanding the players involved in your opposition can help you predict some of the curveballs that might come your way. Later, this will also be useful if you decide to take up magical efforts against your opposition.

Understanding the motivations behind the opposition can seem like an overwhelming task, so let's look at a practical example of how we might approach this.

Let's say that the police in my city have been setting up regular checkpoints at night to test drivers for drugs and alcohol. While keeping drunk drivers off the road is important and a worthy goal, reports have been coming in that the checkpoints have been unfairly targeting marginalized community members, particularly immigrants and folks the police suspect could be undocumented citizens. Citizens are being harassed and intimidated at the checkpoints, causing stress and disorder in our local community.

In this situation, it might seem obvious to look at the police themselves as the main opposition. Even though the racial biases and corruption of the local officers in question are causing the actual distress, we still need to figure out who is *behind* the checkpoints in the first place. I might start by contacting my city council member, requesting information on who ordered the checkpoints. From that conversation I might discover that another city council member was responsible. I might also discover that some problematic neighbors in my community had demanded the checkpoints to resolve their own fear of people who don't look like them. Or I might discover that no local resident or member of my local government leadership was responsible at all. Maybe I learned that it was the chief of police from my local precinct who ordered the checkpoints. So you can see, it doesn't do us any good to assume who may or may not be responsible for something. Doing our due diligence by finding out who exactly is responsible for an injustice is essential before launching into action.

Learning about the people involved on both sides of an issue is just one aspect of our intelligence gathering. Here are a few other factors to consider as you explore and investigate:

* **Past Events.** Has this event or something similar to it occurred in the past? If it has, then learning about that past experience can provide valuable information for your current efforts. What, if anything, was done in the past to resolve this issue? Who were the people involved, and are they still engaged with the issue today? Were there any sort of legal precedents set?

* **Current Events.** Are there any meetings or discussions about the issue such as public hearings, community meetings, or city council meetings? Attending meetings in person or streaming them online can provide you with valuable information about the issue itself and where it's going. If there's a community engagement element to the event, it can also afford you an early opportunity to speak out.

* **Documentation.** You might be surprised by the level of documentation you can find online relating to any number of issues. On the government side, there are Freedom of Information Act (FOIA)

requests you can make. A FOIA request involves a formal plea to a government agency to receive any publicly available documentation about something that occurred in its domain. On the grassroots side, search for any past blog posts, news articles, or interviews about or relating to the issue.

★ **Inside Intel.** Do you know anyone embedded in the core of the situation who can feed you special news and progress reports? Think about people like interns, secretaries, and other staff in an office. If you're very lucky, you might even have a good relationship with a prominent decision-maker who can provide you with special updates. This is very common in the world of politics, but it also happens with community issues, too. You can bet the opposition is doing this, so you might as well do it too.

If you're not the one heading up a particular mission, be sure that you're passing along any intelligence you gather to the person or people running the show. If the issue is on some major national level, then there is probably little you can contribute in terms of intelligence. That said, you can still gather what you know about what's happening and feed that to your community members, peers, and others you know in your various activist circles. One of the major reasons why people are hesitant to get involved with community organizing and activism is that they don't feel like going through the effort of learning about a situation and all of the aspects surrounding it. Being a source of knowledge about a campaign, what's happening with it, and where it's going can be a major motivator for getting others to take action. If you have the motivation to do the work, then it's much more likely that others will step up to pick up the slack on the easy parts.

Here's one small thing I'd like to caution you about as you go about gathering intel: if your research leads you to talk to others involved with the issue, be aware that those same people could be giving your opposition a heads-up about your efforts. Years ago, when it was my job to follow a notoriously abusive circus around the country and document them, a regular part of my duties was to contact city officials to figure out where the circus would be setting up and keeping the animals, and what conditions they might be in. Even though this was usually a straightforward task, there were some civil servants I spoke with in certain cities biased against my efforts who would feed my inquiries back to the circus, letting them know what we were up to. Although this didn't usually mess up my plans to observe and document the conditions of the animals, it sometimes meant that the circus would change its plans so that it would be harder for me to discover where the animals were and make my report. Always be aware of whom you're talking to. This is why cultivating a strong intuition and psychic muscle can be so very useful to our efforts.

Divination for Strategic Planning

Divination, or the art of psychically seeing into the past, present, or future, could really go under the category of intelligence gathering. However, because of how useful and important it can be for the magical activist, I believe it deserves a focused discussion all its own.

Divination has a long history in the world of esoteric politics and magical activism across the political spectrum.

Mystics and mediums have been using psychic power to interfere with things like war and political development for hundreds of years. A fascinating recent example is the Stargate Project, a military intelligence unit established in 1978 to explore the potential usefulness of psychic powers and remote viewing in particular for the U.S. Army. In 1970 U.S. military intelligence discovered that the Soviet Union was spending money and seeing results in research into psychic power. The Stargate Project was a response. The CIA wanted to ensure that the United States wouldn't be left behind if there was anything useful to be gained from the field. Stargate was shut down and declassified in 1995. Although neither mention the program by its specific name, the project was the theme of the 2004 book and 2009 movie *The Men Who Stare at Goats.*

Despite the interesting history of divination used for political ends, most of us won't need to use magic for such glamorous or dramatic results. Divination usually involves very simple practices that can be employed by anyone. My first instructors in witchcraft taught me that every good magic worker should be skilled in at least one form of divination. Whether it's tarot, runes, staring into a bowl of water, or mapping the stars with astrology, the methods by which we can gain a psychic upper hand are nearly unlimited.

Although you can perform your divination at any point throughout a campaign, I typically like to take this step after I have already gained all the mundane information I can. Diviners know that having contextual background beforehand can make greetings easier to interpret and apply to a specific situation. Having your basic intelligence prepared in advance also empowers you to ask the right questions during your reading. Consider divination not as a substitute for intelligence gathering but rather as another layer of information for the work we are already doing as well as a new lens or angle through which to see a situation.

Here's a list of questions to consider when engaging in divination:

* Are there any key pieces of information about this issue that I'm not aware of? If so, what are they?

* Have I identified all of the key people I should know about in this situation, or are there any unknown or underestimated figures I'm not aware of?

* What are the most useful resources I have at my disposal for this situation, and which resources should I rely on the most to carry this issue through to success?

* What are the resources I'm most in need of that I currently lack? What can I do to gain these resources?

* At this stage in my efforts, what will be my biggest obstacle in the near future that I might have the ability to circumvent?

* What types of magic would be most effective for this particular situation?

* How am I approaching this issue personally? Have I done the work of listening to the communities involved and raising the platforms of the people directly affected? Is my mission clear and aligned with my will?

★ What spiritual forces would it benefit me to call upon for the magical aspects of my campaign work?

Feel free to be creative and use your intuition to come up with any number of other questions. As with divination in general, the types of questions you continue to ask will likely be based on the answers you receive as you go along. I prefer to ask no more than three questions during a session so that I can devote the appropriate amount of time to considering the responses, applying them to my situation, and taking any necessary steps that come up as a result of the reading.

If the type of divination you do is some sort of sortilege system—divination involving selecting something out of a grouping, such as tarot, runes, dice, etc.—I've developed a few spreads specifically for activist work that you can use to focus and specify your readings. When you pull your card or other item from the lot, place it in the positions below to frame your reading.

Intelligence Spread

For analyzing and reviewing what your most useful information is, what you don't know, and how the facts of the case could change, use the Intelligence Spread.

WHAT IS THE BEST INFORMATION I HAVE?	WHAT IS SOMETHING I DON'T KNOW ALREADY?	HOW MIGHT THIS INFORMATION CHANGE?

Opposition Spread

For reviewing who your enemies are, what their biggest threat is to your cause, and how you might thwart their efforts, look at the Opposition Spread.

WHO ARE MY OPPONENTS, AND WHAT SHOULD I KNOW ABOUT THEM?	HOW DO MY OPPONENTS MOST THREATEN MY EFFORTS?	HOW CAN MY OPPONENTS BEST BE STOPPED?

Resources Spread

For reviewing what your best resources or set of skills are—who will be most helpful as an ally to the cause, and what new resources you should look out for—sit down with the Resources Spread.

WHAT'S THE BEST RESOURCE CURRENTLY AT MY DISPOSAL?	WHO CAN BEST HELP ME IN THIS WORK?	WHAT FUTURE RESOURCES SHOULD I SEEK?

Some activists may prefer more complex methods of divination like astrology. Astrology is particularly useful for nailing down information about specific dates, events, and the personalities and motivations of the people involved.

Although I personally don't utilize astrology too often in my own personal practice, I do know some magical activists who find it useful and work with it regularly.

Specific things to consider in astrological planning can include the following:

★ Looking at the birth charts of your opposition. This can tell you about their strengths and weaknesses and how they tend to approach decision-making. This can help you interpret what their next steps might be. At the most basic level, consider these three positions:

Sun Sign: The sign the sun was in when you were born. This indicates how someone presents themselves to the world.

Moon Sign: The sign the moon was in when you were born. This indicates the subtle nature of a person, how they feel on the emotional level, and what they keep to themselves more often than not.

Rising Sign: The rising or "ascendant" is determined based on the time of your birth. The rising sign is generally how someone appears to others, whether that impression is true or not.

★ Looking at your own birth chart. It's helpful for everyone to be at least basically familiar with their charts. A personal birth chart can give you insight into your natural strengths and weaknesses. As with all work on personal development and self-knowledge, knowing more about yourself is an important first step in shaping the world around you.

★ Observing the astrological conditions of specific events that will take place during the course of a campaign issue. For example, look to the stars to see what might be influencing something like a planned lobby day or protest. A condition such as a Mars retrograde could warn of an elevated sense of aggression or a stronger focus on malicious intentions. Reviewing things like the placements of planets in aspect to each other, the phases of the moon, and other details can prepare you for the day ahead. There are many simple astrology apps and websites that will highlight the basic influences afoot on a particular day, week, or month. You can even pay attention to things like the planetary hour of a timed meeting or other event to better understand the planetary influences at work.

If you prefer more intuitive methods of divination such as scrying, dream work, and psychometry, you can still use these or similar questions in your reading. In any case, be sure to record the results of your reading so you can continue to refer back to them for consideration throughout your campaign as new events develop.

Becoming Mercurial: Finding Your Voice

As the planet of voice, expression, and the interchange of knowledge, Mercury reminds us of how important it is to find our voice and how to shape it to be the best activists we can be.

When I began my journey into activism, I was extremely shy and remained so years later into my early twenties. Feeling like you don't have a voice or that you don't know how to use it is one of the most common reasons that many people don't even bother getting involved with creating change in the first place. They may think that their voice is either too quiet and insignificant to be heard or they're not eloquent enough to communicate anything of substance. While it's true that some activists have a natural ability to communicate well and make their voices heard, most of us have to learn these skills from the ground up. I'm not just talking about verbal communication such as public speaking. This also relates to writing, emailing, and having discussions with our peers.

Learning the basics of effective communication lends a massive boost to our efficacy. And this isn't just the case for the mundane aspects of our work, but for the magical ones as well. Being an effective communicator is a long-held strength for any effective magician. After all, the whole idea of magic is to speak what we desire into existence. If we can't communicate effectively in the physical world, then how can we hope to do so effectively in the spiritual realm?

Communication and the ability to express our thoughts and ideas clearly and meaningfully are a major topic in the fields of psychology, marketing, business, and political science. Reams have been written about the best ways to share an idea and how to make your voice influential. Dale Carnegie's book *How to Win Friends and Influence People* was first published in 1936, and despite having some problematic aspects for modern readers, the topic of crafting your outward self to make your needs and desires heard and received remains as important today as when it was first put out. Since then many psychologists and communications experts have debated exactly what it takes to be an effective communicator and influencer. Numerous books are dedicated to the topic, and the traits of an effective communicator are hotly debated. Having read many of these types of books myself over the years, I've come to develop my own list of the top strategies and tools I've found most useful, particularly in my activist work:

★ **Active Listening.** Most of us engage in a conversation by saying what we want to say and giving less concern to what is being expressed back to us. It's a natural pitfall of the human condition to prioritize our own selves over others. Active listening is a process by which you focus on what is being said to you first before you worry about immediately forming a response. This is not only helpful for communicating with the communities involved in your issue or your allies, but also for being a better speaker yourself. If you've taken the time to absorb something that someone has told you before you respond, you're going to be in a better position to formulate a response that's on point than if you didn't. Practice active listening with a friend by engaging in a debate about something that you both feel passionate about. After each of you has made a statement, take at least ten seconds to sit and reflect about what they've told you before you respond. Think about how that's changed the flow of the conversation.

★ **Getting to the Point.** Something I had to work on very hard myself in becoming an effective communicator was avoiding rambling on about things. Rambling is easy to fall into. It happens when we're trying to say something while simultaneously thinking about the next thing we want to say, usually with the added fear of being interrupted or the anxiety of not saying something correctly. Before I start speaking or writing about something, I like to establish a set of core statements or talking points in my mind. Talking points are not just for speaking to the media; having them allows you to stay on topic and get to the point quickly. Talking points should be concise, and each one should ideally be no more than two sentences at once. Keep in mind that even though we usually think of talking points for a Q&A or when writing a letter or an email, even in writing a longer text where you can go into more detail, you can still lose people in the weeds.

★ **Being an Expert.** It might seem shallow, but appearing confident and powerful in what you're saying can sometimes be just as important as the ideas you're expressing. In every part of your activism it's important that you portray yourself as an expert on the topic. This doesn't mean being arrogant. Don't pretend that you know things that you don't actually know. However, giving off the feeling that you know what you're talking about will make your ideas and position seem more valid and accepted. If you struggle with confidence, magic is certainly something that can help you. Many of the tools and exercises throughout this book are based on empowering the individual to feel strong and assured. Invoking the energy of the warrior or even activist ancestors who have come before us can be a key part of bringing us out of our shells and into the domain of the expert.

★ **Using the Right Tools.** The mediums you use to communicate play an important role in being seen and heard effectively. If you're putting up visual displays to express your stance or discuss an issue, think about which tools are right for the job. Wearing a pin around your office can be an easy way to express a stance, but only if the message is short and easily read. On the other hand, handing out informational flyers in your community wouldn't go over so well if each flyer only conveyed one sentence. Adjust your message to the medium you use to convey it.

★ **Considering Nonverbal Communication.** Nonverbal communication is a whole area of study unto itself. The way we carry our bodies, move our heads and hands, wrinkle our foreheads, and perform a whole host of other micromotions express specific things about us and what we are saying beyond the words coming out of our mouths. If you're doing an action in person and are the one responsible for communicating a message, be careful to not slouch, fidget, cross your arms, or look away. All of these express uncertainty, fear, or hostility. Standing or sitting tall, having a look of determination and certainty, and appearing comfortable will do more to keep the focus on your message rather than you as the messenger.

With our effective communication strategies in mind, we can turn our attention to the magical ways we can clarify and raise our voices for maximum efficacy. Mercury is the planet that governs the element of air, the powers of speech, and the throat chakra. Allying ourselves with these powers can go a long way in strengthening our voices.

A Spell for Mercurial Voice

The purpose of this short spell is to invoke the airy qualities of Mercury to instill within ourselves a strong voice and clear communicative power. You can wait to work this spell until a time when you think you'll need it, or you can go ahead and do it right now. The more we work with energies like this, the easier it will be to align ourselves with them on a regular basis.

Materials:

Sheet of paper and an orange marker or pen

Small orange or white candle

A sharp tool to inscribe the candle (a pen top will do)

Matches or a lighter

Cord or string

With your tools placed before you, begin to enter a meditative state by focusing on your breath. Breath is the power of air instilled within us and the fuel that powers our voices. As you breathe slowly and deeply, consider the power that air grants us to work our wills in the world.

With your orange marker or pen, draw the alchemical symbol of Mercury largely on your paper:

With your sharp tool inscribe the same symbol on your candle. Set your candle on top of your paper and resume focusing on your breath. Speak the following incantation loudly and confidently:

> *Mercury! Mercury! Mercury!*
> *Hear my voice and send your great winds.*
> *Smooth and quicksilver, strong and clear,*
> *Align within me and settle deep.*

Light the candle. As the flame takes hold, imagine the orangey-silver energy of Mercury rising from the flame and enveloping your body. As you visualize this, slowly chant: *Mercurius.*

Intone the vibration of this word deep within your throat and continue to chant until you reach exhaustion. Then let the candle burn itself down, either onto the paper or within its container.

Later, return to your materials and fold up the paper and bind it with your cord. Carry the resulting charm around with you to reinforce the powers of Mercury you've invoked. I like to carry the charm on my chest like a necklace inside my shirt when I know that my clear voice will be needed for an action.

A Spell to Become Persuasive

Materials:

Cinquefoil (Potentilla reptans)

Hot water

This spell creates an herbal infusion (a tea) out of the cinquefoil plant. Also known as five finger grass due to its characteristic five leaves and its magical "reach," cinque-foil aids in obtaining a commanding presence and helps us extend the reach of our influence.

Fill a tea strainer with the dried or fresh herb and place it in near-boiling water. As the mixture steeps, safely lean your face over it so that the warmth of the vapors can reach your throat and mouth. Say:

> *Flowered grass of five*
> *stir within and be alive*
> *let speech and heart all thrive*
> *flowered grass of five.*

Let the herb steep for about ten minutes and then strain the infusion. Allow it to cool on its own to room temperature. When it has cooled down, use it to wash your hands—so that all you touch is favored by what you want—and face—so that all your words are convincing. Imagine as you wash that these parts of the body are enveloped by a soothing, bright light. Allow your face and hands to air-dry.

If you don't intend to use the infusion right away, you can bottle it up and keep it in the fridge for up to a month.

Building and Joining Communities

There are many things you can do by yourself as an activist, but working within communities can clarify and strengthen the voice of everyone involved. Community work is an important part of strategizing and taking action. Communities not only come together to share and consolidate resources, but they can also lend emotional support, grant us resiliency from burnout, and provide direction on the next steps to take. Activist communities come in many forms. Here are some of the common types you'll encounter:

Large Organizations and Major Nonprofits. Many activists get their feet wet by joining a large organization, typically a nonprofit. Larger organizations act as leaders and focal points for resources, community organizing, and sources of information. The benefit of getting involved with larger organizations is that much of the time we can simply follow their work and take action when called upon to do so. They make it easy—partly because they often employ people—by doing the hard parts for us so that we are free to lend our support either through donations, individual actions, or both. Large organizations can have their downsides too. Some may be critical of them because they feel that the larger the organization, the more separated they are from the voices of the people directly affected by an issue. Getting involved with a large organization is good for people who have extremely limited time to give and want to rely on more vocal and established voices to lead the way.

Small Organizations and Community Groups. Not all established organizations are the huge membership-based nonprofits many of us hear from all the time. Smaller organizations often have fewer resources but tend to be better connected with the core of an issue. This is especially true for issues that operate on a hyperlocal level. An advantage with smaller organizations is that there are usually many ways to get involved, from actions as simple, yet important as giving donations to larger commitments of time like volunteering and even being a volunteer leader. Getting involved with smaller community groups can help you feel like you are having a direct impact, which can go a long way toward keeping you resilient and motivated.

Friend Circles. You don't necessarily need to be involved with a formal organization to build or join a community. A very grassroots way of organizing is to form a friend circle with peers dedicated to taking small actions or joining larger ones. Even though I'm involved with several organizations both large and small, I also have a circle of friends that meet regularly for local letter-writing campaigns. We make our meetings fun by sharing food and drink with each other while we prepare our letters. In my case, most of the people in my little activist friend circle also happen to be witches and magicians themselves. This means we get to add magical elements to our meetings. If you're lucky enough to have magical activist friends yourself, you can formalize meetings like this by turning your friend circle into an activist coven!

Online Communities. Likely the simplest type of group you can find is an online community. Online communities have been a factor since the birth of the internet in bringing people together for taking actions online as well as organizing offline actions. These communities are getting more and more popular as online access becomes increasingly available around the world. In 2011, protests erupted throughout Egypt to overthrow President Hosni Mubarak. The campaign was spearheaded by Egyptian youth who were growing increasingly outraged by issues like police brutality. Due to the strong youth engagement in the campaign, the social media platform Twitter became a powerful tool for what would be a sweeping and effective revolution. Still, online communities do have their downsides. They run the risk of turning people into "armchair activists" or those who think that complaining about something on the internet is the same as creating real and lasting change. They can also become hotbeds of toxicity, harboring trolls and others who latch onto a community with the purpose of bringing them down. If you get involved with an online activist community, just be aware of the pros and cons.

A major advantage of getting involved with a community, whatever its size, is that they help keep our personal egos in check and focus our campaigns on the issues. While I do believe that healthy egos are a good thing, they can sometimes run rampant if we don't have checks and balances. This is particularly vital if you are trying to be an ally to a community rather than a part of the community affected. Our active listening skills come into play here. If you're joining a community as a supportive ally, it is so important to take direction, listen, and act in the ways you're asked to. Know that doing this means you're probably going to miss out on some of the glory of participating in activism. Again, keeping the focus on the issues rather than yourself as the messenger is crucial.

Although being a part of a community can have its challenges, I believe that the benefits to the activist and the causes themselves make it worth the effort. Magicians involved with a magical order or lodge and witches involved with covens know all too well the challenges and benefits involved with group work. Groups give us a sense of identity while also making us feel like we're a part of something larger than ourselves. If you've ever been involved in a moving group ritual, you know how important it is to not only lend your own power and voice to the ritual, but to allow yourself to dissolve within the collective mind of the group. Doing so grants harmony and clear intent to a working, increasing the likelihood that the ritual or spell will be effective.

Egregores and the Group Mind

The local Pagan organization I work with in Washington, D.C., places a strong focus on the power of egregores. An egregore is a type of thoughtform developed either intentionally or unintentionally by groups both magical and mundane. Think of the personal environment at your place of work or within your household. There is a very unique energy for your workplace and within your home that cannot be replicated anywhere else. The way that attitudes and events positively or negatively contribute to those spaces is specific to those environments and the people within them. The unique pattern of energy that is created through these webs of specific people is an egregore.

We intentionally focus on the power of our group egregore as a way to harmonize our actions and keep our community strong, healthy, and compassionate. Being aware of an egregore helps us to stay mindful of things like group dynamics, interpersonal issues, and conflict resolution. Intentionally feeding your community's egregore is important for maintaining a healthy group mind, while also encouraging individuals to maintain a strong and resolute sense of personal identity.

Issues and causes can also have their own egregores. Anytime a group of individuals on either side of an issue focuses their intentions and wills on a topic, a thoughtform is birthed into the world. For better or worse, we are manifesting a type of entity that has the potential to take on its own identity and perform its own actions. Unintentional egregores can become a type of runaway spirit, which can potentially cause chaos and destruction and tear through our cause. The clever magician will identify and work with egregores with intent to maintain control and feed them in ways that are healthy. This is especially useful for egregores born from social justice issues, as the energies involved in their creation are usually strong feelings like passion, commitment, love, and pain.

Declaring a Community Egregore

The purpose of this short meditation is to acknowledge the egregore of a community you're working with or an issue itself. Once you've done that, you will gain a certain type of control and direction over that egregore. After that connection is established, you can actively call upon the egregore in the future to lend power to your magical efforts.

Begin by sitting in meditation and focusing on either your cause or the people involved. Imagine the faces of the people, images of the work being done, and the feelings and emotions that result from that work. Let the feeling and spirit of this group mind wash over you. On every inhale of your breath, take in the essence of what this thoughtform means to you. On every exhale, sense how you are connected to it and part of it yourself.

As you let these images and emotions run through your mind, imagine that they are all connected by a shining and glistening web. This web is the visible part of a great invisible force that connects everyone together: the egregore. Focus your attention on this force, this egregore. Let it flow into you on your inhale, and then add your own power to it with your breath on your exhale. Acknowledge and claim this egregore either with some words of your own choosing or with my Egregore Declaration:

> *I feel the strands of the web.*
> *I am this web.*
> *I see the parts and the whole.*
> *I am this whole.*
> *I listen to the sound of its word.*
> *I am the word.*
> *I speak with its voice.*
> *I am that voice.*
> *I move through its power.*
> *I am that power.*

Imagine the strands of the web connecting the various parts of the egregore are shining brightly from your body. Feel how it breathes as you breathe. Feel how it moves as you move. Know that by recognizing it, you have influence over it.

In the future, when you want to call upon the egregore, simply state the declaration again, feel the strands of the web, and continue with your work whether magical or mundane. Calling upon an egregore before a magical working related to it is a great way to exert influence over the issue. Being connected to the egregore of the LGBTQ community and its issues, I call upon that egregore regularly to fuel my work. Even if you don't choose to actively work magic with any egregores, simply meditating upon them and being aware of the influence of group thoughtforms around you can be enough to sway the needle of change in your direction.

....

Putting It Together: Timelines and Agendas

Knowing the various parts of your strategy, you can start pulling them all together by creating a timeline and an agenda. Timelines can be tricky in activism. Things don't always move along as quickly as we'd like them to, and there may even be times during our efforts when we would like things to slow down a little. A piece of legislation that moves too quickly can leave advocates scrambling to formulate a position and act on it while there is time. But even in those cases having some type of idea of the flow of things will help you prepare as things evolve.

If you're not leading the way, then being aware of the timeline is helpful to stay aware of what you can do to get involved and when. For example, if your work is focused on political issues and following important pieces of legislation, it's crucial to know the various ways in which a bill can move, how long it remains in a particular stage, and when the best times to act are. If you're following a larger organization or community group focusing on this work, then they can usually do the timeline building for you.

Similarly, having an agenda is an important part of keeping yourself organized and responsive to an issue. Many of us are familiar with the idea of keeping an agenda of goals when doing magical work in general: we list our intention, formulate a plan, chart out specific timelines and indicators of success, and spell out exactly what victory would look like. This is the same in our activist efforts.

Here's a sample agenda you can use when formulating your plan of action for both your spiritual and physical efforts. Although this example might not be appropriate for every type of cause and issue, it can get you thinking about your own.

1. Clearly identify the issue, all the parts of it, and what is known about it.

2. Perform a divination to gather additional intelligence.

3. Adjust what you know in Step 1 from the information gathered in your divination.

4. Learn about what resources you have at your disposal and what you'll need.

5. Consult with and stay connected with any appropriate communities.

6. Begin your initial actions and develop a timeline of success.

7. Add power to your physical actions by continuously pairing them with magical ones.

8. Continue to gather intelligence and perform divinations as the issue progresses and changes.

9. Draw attention to the progress of the campaign by using your voice for media attention, peer-to-peer communication, and other mercurial efforts.

10. Regularly learn from the failures and celebrate the successes. Check in with yourself and your communities to avoid burnout.

As you can see, our agenda pairs our magical actions with our physical actions seamlessly. As we move forward in learning about specific methods of offensive and defensive actions, refer back to your strategies, timelines, and agendas to make sure you're still on track. As we launch into action, consider the words of Chinese military strategist Sun Tzu:

> All men can see these tactics whereby
> I conquer, but what none can see is the
> strategy out of which victory is evolved.

Building a Defense

Anything worthwhile is dangerous.

—Victor Anderson

In most forms of activism—at least in the Western world—you're not likely to encounter much danger most of the time. Most avenues of activism are typically simple with little risk. Obviously this depends on the type of action, who is involved, and the goal of the action. Regardless, it's always a good idea to be prepared with a solid defensive system, both on the physical side as well as the magical. This chapter will focus primarily on protection during in-person events like rallies, demonstrations, and marches, but you can apply the techniques and principles to many situations.

Aside from protecting your own self during your campaigns, keep in mind that the campaigns themselves often need protecting. Misinformation from your opponents, bad publicity, and negative propaganda are all things you should think about shielding your campaigns from. As you explore the methods of defense, consider all aspects of your activities and what needs protection.

Situational Awareness

The most basic defensive strategy to begin with is situational awareness. Situational awareness is a whole topic that combines knowledge of the physical space you're in, the people with you, the risk factors, the safety resources available to you, and the offensive resources at your disposal. Simply put, situational awareness is a type of mindfulness. A good magical activist should strive to be mindful at all times, but especially while engaging in an action. There are a lot of variables that can affect an action, and while many of those variables are predictable, some aren't. We want to be prepared for the expected and unexpected alike.

The first part of situational awareness is knowing your surroundings. If you're outside, where are the streets, clearings, and buildings around you? If you're inside, where are the hallways, secured rooms, and, most importantly, the exits? If danger is coming into your space from one direction, are you familiar enough with the environs to exit in the opposite direction, or is there even an exit point in the opposite direction? Be aware of places to hide, where any security might be, and what you can stand behind if you need a barrier. That may seem like a lot to think about, but once you get into the habit, it will come naturally to you to consider your options when you arrive in a space. You can practice by thinking about your surroundings when going to non-activist activities like out to dinner, visiting friends, or even getting your mail.

Next, think about who is occupying this space with you. If you're at a protest, is everyone on your side or is there a counterprotest? Are there law enforcement agents present? Law enforcement carries its own set of safety opportunities and threats depending on who you are and the type of action you're engaging in. If you've brought people with you, be aware of where they are and when. If you know that you'll be separated, have a plan of where to meet and when. Consider that if you're at a large event like a huge march, cell phone reception might not be reliable. If you're at an event with counterprotesters—or you're the one doing the counterprotesting—be aware of how your opposition is acting, if they have any weapons, and the spatial distance between you and them.

Finally, you should be aware of the overall feeling of an event. This is where psychic perception comes in handy when honed and put to practical use. Most of us have experienced situations where something just doesn't "feel" right when we walk into a room. There may not even be any logical explanation for it, but it's like something is hanging in the air—a kind of anticipation or dread.

Last year I attended a political march in my home city of Washington, D.C., with several thousands of people in attendance. There wasn't anything particularly remarkable about the plans for the march or the actions performed along with it. However, a couple of hours into the march, I began to feel an intuitive tugging, like something didn't feel right anymore. It was as if someone had pulled the air out of my stomach. Looking around and taking stock of the situation, I didn't see any obvious reason to feel anxious. I pressed on a bit longer, but as I had a sore foot anyway, I stepped away from the march and ducked into a coffee shop to rest. Hours later I found out that shortly after I stepped off the march route, riot police rounded up dozens of people in the section I was in and carted them off—without cause—into police vans.

In that situation there wasn't anything I specifically did before the march to up my psychic senses. Keeping a sharp intuition is something that one should carefully craft over time. That said, there are a few strategies I now employ to fine-tune psychic power before performing an action.

Activist's Intuition

Consider the following exercises and tips not only while preparing for an action, but also as part of your daily practice. Cultivating situational intuition is a skill that can come in handy when you least expect it.

Breathing in a Surrounding. Calm your mind and focus on your breath. On your inhale imagine that the psychic information from the space around you is being pulled in on your breath. The sights, smells, sounds, and feelings are all being sucked into your body and integrating with your entire being. Doing this, you infuse your surroundings with your own essence. This will give you the upper hand in sensing anything unusual that enters the space around you whether you're aware of it or not.

Psychic Scanning. When entering a space, allow your eyes and vision to relax. Turn your head to the left and slowly gaze upon the landscape as you turn to the right, taking in as much visual detail as possible. Then shift your head back to the left and do the same thing with your eyes shut. What do you remember? What has become fuzzy? It is likely that the first few times you do this you won't recall much if you're not in a very familiar place. But doing this exercise repeatedly will enable you to perform it very rapidly with increased accuracy. Being able to psychically scan an environment quickly will sharpen your senses and keep your mystical third eye wide open.

Psychometry. Psychometry is the practice of reading the energetic residue left on objects both inert and alive, including humans. Practicing psychometry will enable you to literally read the room and rapidly grab information from the space. This is extremely useful in situations like meeting with your local politicians in their office. Practice psychometry by taking an object in your hand that has enormous meaning to someone else. Wedding rings, a favorite sweater, a long-worn shoe, or a pair of glasses are all great choices. As you hold the object in your hands, imagine a blank screen in your mind's eye. Slowly and without forcing it, allow shadows and shapes to form on the screen. Gently allow them to come into focus and play out before you like a movie. They will probably show images from the person's very recent past, when the psychic imprint of their energy was recently strongest. Talk to the person about what you're seeing and have them record it in some way. Test your accuracy afterward. This is another method that only gets better with time, so don't worry if you're pretty far off in the beginning. Years ago, I practiced psychometry as an activist while meeting with a local legislator's staff in their office on a particularly disagreeable issue. I knew I was going to have to convince them of my position and could use some help in gaining the upper hand. When I shook the staffers' hands, I made sure to do it rather slowly, focusing on the vibrations of their hand imprinting with mine. As we sat down and prepared for discussion, I "read" that energy to figure out the best way to engage in the discussion. I had planned on coming in with a very aggressive demeanor, but the staffers' vibrations indicated that they were having a rough day and would respond better to a gentler approach. I adjusted my plan on the spot, and the discussion was better for it.

While cultivating an activist's intuition, remember to keep all of the physical items of importance in mind too. Over time, you should feel comfortable with incorporating all of these strategies when engaging in any effort. Doing so will leave you well prepared for the next steps ahead.

Protecting Yourself at Marches, Rallies, and Other Events

Most in-person demonstrations are peaceful and coordinated, whether large or small. Still, that doesn't mean that some participant won't make a mess of things or that an ill-informed—or ill-intentioned—law enforcement officer won't do so as well. If we're practicing our situational awareness, we already expect the unexpected. Protecting yourself at events ranges from the simplest considerations imaginable all the way into things that many activists aren't ever likely to encounter often, if ever. First, let's start with the basics: your own body.

When going to an in-person action, it's important to get the basics of your body right first. Get a good night's sleep, stay hydrated, wear comfortable footwear, and dress for the weather if you're going to be outdoors. If you don't keep these basic body considerations in mind, your stamina is going to tank, and you're not going to be as helpful to your cause as you could be. A good warrior is one who takes stock of their physical limitations as well as their strengths.

Remember that everyone's body is different and keep in mind that because of this, you don't necessarily need to do what everyone else is doing. For example, think of an hours-long standing protest in the hot summer sun. An elderly person with a thinner frame is not going to hold up as long in those conditions without risking their health compared to a twenty-year-old at the peak of their physical fitness. In speaking for myself, I know that with my terrible posture and muscle issues, it's best for me to limit standing to just a few hours at an event and then figure out a seated way to help after that. Additionally, folks in wheelchairs may need to think about accessibility in terms of a marching terrain or entrances into buildings. Hopefully the organizers of the action have thought about accessibility ahead of time, but that's not always the case.

While discussing bodily considerations, we should also look at the issue of profiling by law enforcement officials. In an ideal world, exercising our rights to make our thoughts and feelings known should be protected without infringement, but this isn't always the case. This is especially true for marginalized people along with people who fall into younger age categories. If you're younger, you might be unfairly targeted because you could be considered more of a threat than an elderly activist. And sadly, having black or brown skin means being unfairly targeted due to the internal racism that continues to plague so many nations. Keeping this in mind, take care of yourself and keep your body safe. The only thing more important than the work you're doing is you.

A Brief Introduction to Physical Body Shielding

Before we dive into the magical aspects of body shielding, it's worth it to cover some universal tips on shielding the body in the unlikely event of a physical threat at an in-person action. Entire books have been written for activists about protecting their bodies at marches and protests. Since most readers of this book aren't likely to attend events where physical injury is any serious threat, I won't go too deeply into it here. Still, I have always believed that being prepared is the best defense and anything that can happen, might happen.

When an activist is attacked at a demonstration or other event, it is not usually because they're looking for trouble. Most often it seems to be instigated by angry supporters of an opposing issue or ill-trained and aggressive law enforcement.

The first way to respond to the threat of violence is to avoid it if at all possible. At a march, for example, you can try turning back in the other direction if you see violent activity in front of you. You can also break off into another direction down a less crowded street if that's an option. Abandon any signs or banners you might be carrying so you can try to blend in with the surroundings.

If you can't get away and an attacker is upon you, the standard advice is typically to continue to try and escape. If this still proves impossible, it is usually recommended that you protect your head and vital organs by curling up with your knees tucked in and your arms covering your head. Damage done to the legs and arms isn't likely to be as much of an issue as anything on your head or torso. And again, if the opportunity to escape presents itself during the episode, take it. In the unlikely event of violence during protests, any attacks are often instigated very quickly and break up just as fast.

In case it's not obvious: seek medical attention if you need it and assist others if you can by calling for help.

Conjuring Spirits of Defense

There's an old saying, "a witch is never alone." This is great news for the activist witch because in the world of the advocate, you're often only as strong as your comrades in the work. While for most people that means relying only on communications and media work to defend a campaign from the opposition, it means so much more for the magic workers among us.

When working for progress and change, a big mistake that some activists make is thinking that one step forward for an issue means that you'll always be stepping forward. The victories we win, the progress we make, and the little changes we secure require constant defense. Consider the major victory for marriage equality in the United States in 2015 conferred by *Obergefell v. Hodges*. This victory in the Supreme Court of the United States instantly brought marriage rights access to all couples on every inch of the United States. Unfortunately, people who oppose equal rights for LGBTQ people immediately got to work to undermine those rights in states all over the country. We saw courthouse officials challenging their obligation to offer marriage licenses, states attempting to pass "marriage definition" bills limiting the reach of the case, and a whole host of anti-LGBTQ legislation created to chip away at the rights of all queer Americans. This sort of backlash is very common, and although marriage is an example of it on a broad scale, it occurs for just about every issue.

Spirits of defense can be conjured forth and "stationed" during your work to protect the progress of your campaign, to safeguard people engaging in in-person street activism, and for just about any other reason you might use a helping hand. The activist witch might call upon the aid of ancestral spirits, spirits of the land (which would be particularly suitable for environmental causes), animal spirits, and otherworldly spirits such as demons and angels. There are also spirits of stones and plants appropriate for this type of work.

Conjuring a spirit typically involves multiple steps that can be shorter or longer depending on the type of spirit you're calling and what you're asking them to do:

1. **Preparing to meet them.** I always suggest that it is worth it to meet the spirits halfway. It is helpful to enter a trance or some other kind of ritual space so the spirit has an easier time accessing you and your request. This is often done through erecting a magic circle, but you could also do it by going to some liminal place like a crossroads, bridge, or sacred site at some liminal time such as twilight, dawn, dusk, midnight, a full moon, etc.

2. **Signaling.** You must first signal the spirit to get their attention. Some kind of invocation tailored to them

should do the trick. Tracing sigils and signs associated with their nature or presenting objects, colors, and scents known to be favored by them are other options. Ideally, you might combine multiple methods to signal to the spirit that you'd like to work together.

3. **Agreement and direction.** With the spirit signaled and hopefully paying attention to your request, you enter into some kind of agreement with them. Most of the time this can be as simple as giving them an offering and promising more if they carry out your goal with success. For example, I might present a bottle of whiskey for my grandfather, pouring half of it in an offering bowl and then letting him know that if he can complete my request, the other half will be waiting. This may seem conniving, but the spirit world understands these types of trades and responds well to them. The direction or instruction is given during the agreement. You'll want to be very clear with your ask and set a timeline. Be as specific as possible.

4. **Follow-through.** Finally, don't forget to hold up your end of the bargain, and definitely be sure to thank the spirits involved in your work.

The more you work with specific spirits, the friendlier to your goals they tend to become. Forging spirit alliances is much like nurturing any kind of friendship. When you put the time and work in, doing things for one another when you can, you will reap the benefits.

Contacting the Ancestral Spirits of Activism

My favorite spirits to work with on my causes are those deceased humans who have also done the work themselves. Spirits don't stop caring about the things they were concerned about in life after they cross to the other side. Most of the time I've engaged with the spirits of activists, I've actually found that they tend to be equally as passionate and interested in seeing their work carried on by future generations. Having the belief that it is up to humans to be proactive to seek out change, activist ancestors of humanity are often very willing to lend their aid to a cause, whether for offense or defense.

While you can consider contacting any of the magical activists discussed in the History and Culture section of this book, I recommend asking the people who were deeply involved in an issue and experienced some success with it. I call these people "ancestors" not because you need to have any familial connection to them, but because they are ancestors of humankind. While making your choice, think about the disposition of the activist while they were alive. What was their personality like? Did they function well in teams or did they prefer to do their work solo much of the time? Were they generally calm or did they have a fiery temper? All of these qualities can influence the type of energy the spirit may bring to your project, so learn what you can about their life, their personality, and their activism.

To begin the work, place an image of the person on an altar setup. You can also accompany that with objects and colors they liked in life, if you're aware of what those things might be. Try to make the space look lovely and appealing, possibly adding flowers and candles to the arrangement. Plants, flames, and dishes of water are all sources of vital life force energy that spirits can draw from to make their presence felt in our world.

Next, relax before the altar space and allow your gaze to rest on the altar as you breathe slowly and deeply. Allow your thoughts to settle as you focus your attention only on your breath and the image of the ancestor. As you enter a state of meditation, allow the space around you to soften and fall away in your mind. Imagine that in this space, it is only you and the presence of the spirit you're calling forth.

Begin to whisper their name as you stare at their image. Add details about their life and craft to your own invocation tailored to them. For example, in calling the great artist and occultist Pamela Colman Smith, I might say:

> *Pamela Colman Smith*
> *Pamela . . . Pamela . . . Pamela*
> *Daughter of Charles Edward Smith*
> *Daughter of Corinne Colman*
> *Of London, Manchester, Kingston, Brooklyn,*
>   *and Cornwall*
> *Artist, magician, and writer.*
> *I honor your work, legacy, and life.*
> *Enter this space if it is your will*
> *And take notice of this work.*
> *Pamela Colman Smith, I welcome you.*

At this time, present any offerings you have prepared such as lighting incense, pouring a libation out, or placing food on a plate in front of the photographs.

Breathing slowly and deeply, stay quiet and still and see if you can feel the spirit's presence in the room. Notice any signs like a flickering candle, a wave of sudden hot or cold in the room, or even just an internal sense of their presence. Then proceed to make your request.

If your working is focused entirely on making a request of the ancestral spirit, you can simply talk to them and tell them what it is that you'd like. If it is part of a larger working like a spell or ritual, you may ask them to attend to the rite and lend any influence they're able to. I like to write out my request on a sheet of paper and place that under the offerings I've presented, along with their photo. If you're making a specific agreement with the spirit such as offering a future gift if they agree to help you out, you can also do that now.

Be sure to complete the working by saying thank you.

Spirits of Place and of the Land

Nonhuman spirits who inhabit specific places are of particular importance for the magical activist because our work is often focused around important events. Whether it is a vote in Congress, the city council passing a new law, or an organization getting approved for community funding, we often center our activist work around occurrences that require our constant attention.

These events often happen at central locations like government institutions, community centers, or directly in the streets. As these events unfold, their energy leaves imprints in the land which merge into the spirits of those places. We can look to the Roman idea of the genii loci (spirits of place) to see how these types of spirits were honored and why they were so important. If the genii loci are happy, then the people who inhabit that space are happy. In the case of the home, the genii loci help ensure that a family has enough food to eat and that their house stays secure. In the case of a government office, the spirits of place can keep the peace and foster communication and agreement between parties and constituents.

Sometimes spirits of place can be volatile and chaotic if something traumatic happened there. Still, even these spirits can be called upon to work to prevent similar situations, and partnering with these spirits can actually heal the land and benefit the spirits who are there. This can make these spirits even more agreeable to your work. For example, spirits of the land on a battlefield might be called upon by the activist witch to help prevent a battle or to lessen the damage if a battle feels inevitable.

Spirits of the land can be particularly helpful in setting up defenses for in-person events as well as protecting physical places and maintaining peace in those spaces. For example, an important election in your area could benefit from asking the spirits of the polling locations to step in and keep an eye on things.

While spirits of the land are often indifferent to the politics of humans, they can be cajoled into lending their aid for your specific work. As with most types of spirits, you'll do this through forging a long-term relationship with them and giving them regular offerings. Consider cleaning the land of pollution and debris as an offering, along with leaving food and drink that will organically decompose on the earth.

A Rite for Defensive Land Spirits

This simple working is designed to draw the attention of the spirits of the land to protect a space, event, or specific people inhabiting the spirits' domain. I like to perform rites like these ahead of a large event like a big march, but you can apply it on a much smaller scale for just about any defensive purpose you could think of.

Materials:

Small loaf of whole bread

Jug of springwater

Stand at the general center of the space you wish to have protected. Allow your breathing to slow and let your personal attention turn to the natural land around you. What does the earth feel like beneath your feet? What does the wind feel like on your skin? What types of animals can you hear moving through the space? Take in all of these observations as you merge your full attention with the land. When you feel truly connected to the site, speak the invocation:

> *Spirits of space; the east, south, north, and center,*
> *Of flora, fauna, faerie, and stone,*
> *I call your favorable attention unto me.*
> *A steward of the land cries out to you*
> *Awaken for the defense of this your domain*
> *And the people within.*
> *Hail to your holy names!*

Move to the far north of the space and walk clockwise, tearing off pieces of bread and placing them discreetly as you walk. Also pour out the springwater, particularly over stones and at the roots of any trees. Walk slowly and solemnly, feeling the impact of your gifts and sensing if they're being received with any notice.

When you return again to the north, sit in quiet meditation for a time, continuing to focus deeply on the land and any buildings on it. When you feel satisfied, turn and walk away from the site, not looking back (looking behind you after calling spirits to a space is considered distrustful and offensive to the spirits).

If the spirits of the land were satisfied with your call and gifts, they should set to work with their own way of defending the space against chaos, attack, and harmful influence.

....

Your Own Guardian Spirits

As you build relationships with the spirits of defense, it is natural that some of them will stay at your side for your general daily protection. It is also helpful to actively ask spirits who are particularly friendly to you to become your personal guardians, whether you're doing activist work at the moment or not. Being well-guarded as an activist is important for your own general well-being, both for keeping you safe from attack as well as the preservation of your own positive mental and emotional state. To an activist, emotional burnout is sometimes the greatest threat.

When it comes to your own personal protection, there are a number of specific strategies you can employ to foster and maintain the presence of protective spirits around you:

★ Wear a talisman that holds the image (such as a photo if it's a human spirit) or symbol (for nonhuman spirits) of the guardian. There's no need to purchase fancy jewelry. Simply carrying it on you is just fine.

★ Expanding upon the above, make a fetish of the spirit to carry with you. A spirit fetish is a hand-crafted object meant to represent the actual body of the spirit and may contain things associated with it. These can be made of clay, cloth, wood, or any number of materials. Consider them portable statues.

★ Make a regular offering before you leave for the day, and ask your favored spirits to come along. As part of my regular morning practice I will light a stick of incense that burns while I'm getting ready. As I set it alight, I say something like "Smoke is the gift of air and may it carry my devotion to [spirit] through this blessed day."

★ Chant the names of the spirits as you walk or do an activity for an added layer of personal protection.

★ Privately toast to the spirits' names at meals.

With spirits charged with your own personal protection, it is important to remember that you must actively ask them to come to your defense on a regular basis. Some spirits will specifically avoid interfering with your life unless you request they do so. Angelic spirits in particular are often said to completely avoid any human interaction unless they're called upon. Don't be afraid to ask.

Symbols and Sigils of Defense

Symbols (universally known images) and sigils (symbols of personal significance) are an easy and convenient way of tapping into great amounts of energy quickly and with very little effort or maintenance. Symbols work by plugging into the current of energy they're associated with, like entering a computer password to access a specific program.

Defensive symbols can be worn as jewelry, painted on objects and walls, traced in the air with your fingers, written on paper, and even baked into food! Their versatility makes them one of my favorite methods for employing strategic magic.

For the activist, defensive symbols can be discreetly inscribed on campaign materials, displayed in signs and banners, and placed on websites and other digital spaces. A protective symbol can help prevent a website from getting hacked, be placed on someone during an event to keep them safe, or be put on literature and other media to protect the integrity and movement of a message.

There are thousands of known protective symbols. With the constraint of space I won't produce very many here, so consider once again getting creative and looking at different symbols you can pick up and put to use for your work. Below are some of my favorite symbols for defense that I regularly use for my own activism work. They've served me well over the years, and I'm sure they'll do the same for you.

Raised Fist. This symbol first appeared as a logo for the Industrial Workers of the World, a labor union most active around 1917. It's been used for the past century to represent solidarity, the act of standing in collective unity in defense of your fellow citizens. It is my favorite protective activist symbol because it represents the courage required to make the world a better place and the great defensive power that activists have when we're united in a common cause.

Pentagram. The pentagram is an ancient symbol associated with the goddess Venus, the sea, witchcraft, and the elements of nature. This five-pointed star without a circle around it resembles a human body with all the limbs outstretched and acts as an effective personal protective symbol, specifically for safeguarding the physical body. I like to wear a pentagram at marches and rallies where I'm exposed to large crowds.

Saturn. Saturn is the planet of karma, protection, cycles, and deep lessons. Use the symbol of Saturn to call upon the protective qualities of this planet. Draw it in black or deep purple and intone its name by vibrating the name out loud. Saturn is associated with the angel Cassiel, the archangel of the oppressed and downtrodden. Use the Saturn symbol while calling upon Cassiel during defensive spirit conjurations.

Inverted Triangle. The triangle represents the three realms of land, sea, and sky and the worlds of above, below, and center. Used by the classic western magicians, it's known for containing dangerous spirits and channeling energy. In modern times, it's associated with the LGBTQ movement as a symbol of solidarity with queer peoples, because it was used to designate accused homosexuals during World War II. The inverted triangle also resembles a shield.

Eyes. The eye has a very long history of protecting the body among many ancient cultures. There are several variations to it, but it always involves a bold-looking eye staring straight ahead. The idea is that the eye is always keeping a lookout when you might be too distracted to pay attention yourself. For the activist, the eye of protection can also be used to defend communities that are often overlooked by society.

Shield. Magic partly works on the idea that "like attracts like," which means the image of an actual shield is a simple but time-honored protective symbol. My favorite use of the shield symbol is to customize it by adding other images, words, and symbols on its face. Shield symbols can also be used to rally a group by invoking the spirit of the warrior archetype. It helps people feel empowered to take the risks required to stir up great change.

Algiz Rune. *Algiz* means "Elk" and is the Norse rune representing guidance and higher power. It's traced from the bottom up, pulling up energy from the Earth and forging it into a protective shield. You can repeat the rune and form a pattern, creating an impenetrable wall. Although runes have been wrongly appropriated by some hate groups, it's important to not let the forces of oppression take over these beautiful and powerful symbols.

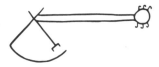

Vatnahlífir. This interesting symbol is one of the Icelandic magical staves and was known to protect against drowning. Vatnahlífir can be used by activists to protect against the metaphorical "drowning" of burnout. Try tracing it into your bathwater to relax and refresh yourself when the weight of the world feels like it's getting to be too much to handle.

Setting Wards

Wards are energetic barriers erected once and relied upon to stay and regularly protect a person or place without much follow-up. The benefit of setting up a ward is that once it's up, all you need to do is refresh it with a boost of energy every once in a while. In the busy life of an activist, setting personal wards can help filter out a bit of the heaviness that bears down on a person when they're engaged in the work of constantly taking on injustice.

To set up a basic ward, you'll focus on pulling from a strong, stable source of energy from the natural world, which remains connected and running at all times. Through visualization, intention, and breath, you'll program it to do specifically what you need it to do.

In this example working we'll focus on setting up a personal ward, but you can easily adapt the steps to ward a place instead.

Stand tall with your posture straight and your feet planted firmly, arms resting at your side. Close your eyes and breathe slowly and deeply, imagining your body becoming larger and larger, until it grows beyond the space of the room and into an impossibly giant statue, rising high above any buildings. While in this position of strength and might, point your right hand to the ground and "pull" up golden and shining bars of energy from the center of the Earth. As you pull them up, imagine them stretching above, your head and extending into the heavens above where they become implanted and firm. Do this over and over until the shining bars of light form a cage all around you.

Next, look up and point your right hand to the sky. See the sun (or imagine it) above you and pull down shining bars of golden light, anchoring them into the Earth below you. Do this repeatedly, forming another layer of caged light set into the ground.

Focus on your breath as you feel the bars of light shining brightly around you. While they glow strongly with the hot light of the celestial bodies, the light is also soft and flexible, burning away harmful influences as they approach you but allowing helpful influences to pass through without interruption.

Finally, form a clear thought in your mind with your specific intention for this particular ward. Is it to prevent excess stress from reaching you? Is it simply to protect your physical body? Whatever it may be for, have a clear vision of what that means for you. To connect the intention to your ward, take a deep breath in and then loudly vibrate "AAAAAH."

As you vibrate this sound, imagine the bars of light thickening and forming a reflective wall all around you. You can intone the sound repeatedly until you're satisfied with how the ward solidifies. It is done.

Every few weeks or so, refresh the wards by pulling up more Earth energy and pulling down more celestial energy. Intone the vibrating sound once more to solidify the new energy.

In addition to protecting yourself with wards, you can also set wards around a location, which is particularly useful at protest and rally events where the energy might feel wild and chaotic.

Getting good at ward setting eventually means you can spend a little less time on personal protection and a little more time on getting your true work done. With so many defensive strategies in place, we can begin to work on our offense and actively start manifesting changes in the world around us.

Building an Offense

Let your plans be dark and impenetrable as night, and
when you move, fall like a thunderbolt.

—Sun Tzu, *The Art of War*

Activists are typically painted as either too aggressive or not aggressive enough. Our opponents will make us appear as if we are unreasonable bullies, pushing forward a radical agenda before the world is ready to receive it. Much of the antiactivist propaganda from the past couple of centuries is designed to make advocates of progressive causes seem disconnected from the reasonable and compassionate everyday citizen. This type of othering is often very effective because it means activists must spend more time and resources defending themselves and their cause rather than pushing it forward.

On the other end of the spectrum, sometimes our fellow comrades for a cause will say that we're not aggressive enough, not willing to get down and dirty with strategies for offense.

This will always be the fate of people trying to create change in the world, whether a civilian activist, a politician, a spiritual leader, or just about anyone with a public voice and platform pushing an agenda. This tug-of-war can paralyze activists and leave them unsure of what to do and how to move forward. It can make us feel as if we should become quiet and reserved about our causes, worrying about shaking up the status quo and offending potential allies. While there is certainly something to be said for bringing compassion and active listening to our work, we must be careful to not lower our voices to the point they are rendered ineffective.

After building a defense and bringing our strategy to the table, the time comes to act and carry out our plan of attack, and we have to be ready to act regardless of the naysayers. You may be wondering why I would use aggressive terms like "planning an offense" and "attacking." I don't shy away from speaking in ways that appear aggressive on the surface because this work can often be aggressive. Activism isn't always about gently educating and waiting for change. Sometimes it is about pushing your obstacles away and demanding that change occur by force. To me this also encompasses the spirit of magic itself: while prayer is an invitation to state our case and hope for the best, magic is a tool that allows us to become the decision-makers and rearrange the environment around us according to our will.

Preparing for Sustainable Battle

As you charge into action with all of your resources and strategies behind you, you'll want to keep an eye on your energy levels both spiritually and physically. Ensuring you'll have the resources to take action has already been covered, but it's equally important to sustain those resources throughout our actions.

Over the course of a campaign it's important to make sure all of your basic needs will be met as well as you can:

* **Food.** Eat healthy food that makes you feel strong and fortified. Eating well not only helps sustain your physical body, but can also support your mental health and spiritual bodies. For physical events that will last a while, bring snacks.

* **Water.** Hydration is always a major concern, but especially so for the busy activist. Becoming dehydrated can affect your quality of sleep, stress level, digestion, energy level, mood, and a host of other things. For events like marches and rallies where you might be outside for a while, bring water bottles.

* **Sleep.** Activism can be stressful, and getting the right amount of sleep for your body is crucial to preventing burnout. Everyone requires different amounts of sleep, so be familiar with what your own body needs. Pay particular attention to getting good sleep the night before an action.

* **Time Management.** Don't take on more than you can handle. If there are still things that need to get done, delegate them if possible. You don't have to attend every event or hold every banner.

These are all essential factors that go into preventing burnout. Although *burnout* is a wide-reaching term, generally it's the experience of feeling exhausted, fed up, or even physically ill after a period of overextending yourself. Burnout can begin as inconspicuously as simple fatigue or anxiety. Left unchecked, it can cause a person to feel completely detached, like they need to shut down, or to actually become ill.

Burnout most often occurs in the middle or toward the end of a campaign, which is why we need to place such a strong focus on fortifying ourselves in advance. When we set ourselves up to be sustainable, we'll have the energy reserves needed to begin manifesting.

To Go

As discussed earlier in the book, the Witch's Pyramid, or Four Powers of the Sphinx, is sometimes portrayed with an additional axiom at its peak: "To Go." This is the final action point of our work after Knowing (learning the basics), Willing (developing a strategy), Daring (moving from strategy and into action), and Keeping Silent (building a defense). With a stable and powerful base, we should be more than ready to project our power into the world and see it through to manifestation.

While the base points of the pyramid are connected to the physical elements of earth, air, fire, and water, To Go is associated with spirit as the force that animates all things and without which all matter would be dead and immobile. The magician knows that all matter contains spirit and tapping into the spirit of matter is a vital part of giving your magic the lift it needs to start moving.

Enchantment

To enchant something is to instill a power within it by tapping into its power and infusing it with the power you've generated. When we examined different methods of raising energy for our goals, we looked at just a few of the many different ways this can be done. Now it's time to project that power into our missions and goals.

When you're ready to take an action like attending a protest, for example, you can actively enchant the event itself to be a space for maximum efficacy. Working with a space or event is already familiar to us, as we looked at doing this for protective strategies in the chapter on building up a defense. For our offensive strategy, we can do similar things to draw attention to our goal and attract the beneficial things we need.

Just like using situational awareness to see how vulnerable you might be at an event, you can look at the setup of an event or situation and figure out how to make it stronger, more visible, and more empowered.

In the example of an event, first look at the details of the event itself. Is it in a highly visible area? Are media present? What is the turnout like? Is the visual setup of the event engaging and does it display a clear message? If the answer to any of those questions is no, then that's a good place to focus for enhancement purposes.

If you're at an event, approach the edge of the space if you can do so without drawing obvious attention to yourself. If that isn't possible, simply retreat to some area where you're less visible. Even a restroom will do in a pinch. With your mind's eye, begin to sense the center and circumference of the space as you tune in to the energy of the event and the space it occupies. See if you can sense the level of energy inhabiting the space. Does the space seem friendly to your goals, in opposition of them, or neutral? Use your intuitive skills to feel things out. If the space feels oppositional, this practice will bring it into a state of positive favor.

Touch the space in some way, whether by placing your hand on the ground or wall, firmly planting your feet and becoming aware of them, or sitting on the ground. Think of how the space feels versus what you'd like it to feel like and then visualize the change you'd like to experience. If the event has a low turnout, feel as though the space is buzzing with a massive crowd. If it seems like it's not getting the attention it deserves, imagine the entire space is shining brightly, like a beacon that can been seen from the farthest reaches of space. If the speakers seem like they are lacking energy or forcefulness, aid them by charging up the space with feelings of vitality, courage, and fearlessness.

When working with objects like a letter you're about to mail to a decision-maker or a sign you'll hold in a march, you can use a similar method. As you hold the object in your hands, breathe into it while intensely focusing on the impressions you'd like it to give off. In the example of the letter, you might breathe the intention of "persuasion" into it.

In the case of a physical meeting where your presence is meant to have an influence on someone or several people, you can enchant yourself. Glamour, or the magical art of influencing/altering your own physical or spiritual presence, can play a critical part in having your ideas heard, absorbed, and implemented by those around you. While some might question the ethics of glamour being used in this way, consider the choices you make every day to influence the people around you. Dressing well for a job interview, putting on some nice perfume before a date, or selecting a tie color that exudes confidence are all little mundane ways that we cast glamours upon ourselves all the time.

For a basic glamour enchantment, sit in front of a mirror and stare deeply at your own face. Examine every line, feature, and color, learning every detail as deeply as you can. Once you've taken in the full sight of yourself, gaze deeply into your own eyes while letting them relax ever so slightly. While holding your gaze, imaging your form shifting and shimmering around you. Your form itself might change in this visualization, or it could just be the vibrations around you. Either way, use your imagination to shape-shift into a form that strongly represents what you're trying to convey. If I'm preparing to go to a meeting where I need to influence a decision-maker, I might imagine the form of a powerful negotiator. If I'm going to a protest, I might call up the image of someone who is known or was known in the past for being a master organizer. You can call upon any of the images of the activist ancestors, someone living, or even someone or something you've completely made up! The power is in the vibrational energy you're assigning to your new form. Once you feel like the energy has settled over your image, move forward to do your work. Glamour magic doesn't tend to last for very long, so you may need to repeat this exercise each day you intend to use it.

Magical Thoughtforms

Creating a magical thoughtform is an old skill that's been put into practice for magical activism for quite some time. A thoughtform is typically a kind of entity created and empowered by the magician, imbued with a specific mission and intelligence, and then sent out to do the work. These are artificial beings, meaning they are created entirely from scratch through the will and imagination of the magician. As artificial beings, they tend to be easy to program, control, and empower. They are, in essence, an extension of your own will imbued with the goals you instill within them.

When Dion Fortune set about her work of repelling the Nazi invasion of Britain with a series of visualizations, she asked her magical order to imagine shadowy figures patrolling the coastlines. Thoughtforms can come in many shapes and manifestations such as Fortune's shadowy figures, magical creatures, animals, humanoid forms, or even machinelike figures similar to androids. The form is an important choice since you'll want to have an emotional connection to it that inspires you and triggers a strong association with what you're trying to accomplish.

Thoughtforms can play an enormously helpful role in building up our offense. Think of your thoughtforms as your own personal army, marching into battle with direct orders from their general—you. When their mission is complete, they can either dissipate or be returned to you. Either option can be programmed into the thoughtform when you create it.

For our campaign work, we can use thoughtforms for anything from protecting us while we're out on the streets in a rally to retrieving information, undermining the efforts of our opponents, and just about anything else you can think of for an extra set of astral hands. I like to assign a thoughtform for the full length of a specific campaign and then adjust its course or mission as I go. At the end after we've won or lost, I'll dissolve it and move on to the next thing. The power of a thoughtform is based strongly on the theme or mission you have charted out, so most magic workers avoid recycling them for new things that they weren't created for.

The actual process of creating a thoughtform can be simple or complicated based on the complexities of what you're trying to do. Dion Fortune's instructions of just visualizing the figures would certainly be among the more basic methods. Others, often from more formalized systems of magic, require a great deal of ritual, symbolism, and steps. My favorite methods are somewhere in the middle: more involved than a simple visualization yet not requiring major ritual work either.

Creating a Thoughtform

Materials:

Sketch pad

Small wood or stone container

Small quartz crystal

Before you gather your materials, you need to determine your precise goal and what you would like your thoughtform to accomplish. While it's not necessary to write it all down, I usually find that helpful for clarifying my will and imagining exactly what I want.

With your sketch pad, roughly draw out what you imagine you want your thoughtform to look like. Don't worry: you don't need to be a talented artist. A simple sketch is what's important for taking your mental idea from the astral world into the physical. As you draw out what you'd like your thoughtform to look like, really use your imagination. Begin to flesh out the character of the thoughtform itself: the temperament you'd like it to have, the level of aggression or peacefulness you'd like it to embody, and even physical things like how you'd like it to intervene. Developing your own mythos behind your thoughtform will lend it a body of power that will sustain it on its mission.

With your sketch all drawn out and the profile of your thoughtform set up in your mind, gaze on what you've drawn and begin to imagine what it would look like if it were standing right before you. You might like to close your eyes to conjure up a strong visualization of the being.

Take up your crystal—it's quartz for projection, manifestation, and containment—and visualize a point of light containing the image of your thoughtform projecting from your forehead and into the crystal. Allow the light to build and build within the crystal. When no more light will project into the stone, declare the birth of the thoughtform in the physical world and give it a name:

> *I name you, [thoughtform name]!*
> *Be a being of thought and form.*
> *Your will is mine and unto me*
> *Within the crystal now be born*
> *And I a parent unto thee.*
> *Be my agent in the skies*
> *And travel fast in any sea.*
> *Be attentive to my cries*
> *And carry out my every plea.*
> *Oh servant of my inner light,*
> *Be resound 'cross every plane.*
> *Body, force, and form take flight*
> *and answer to your given name!*
> *[thoughtform name yelled x3]!*

Take deep breaths and slowly breathe life force energy into the crystal, nearly to the point of becoming dizzy from the effort.

The crystal serves as not only a place of gestation for your thoughtform, but also a house for it when it's not on a mission. When you are not using the crystal, store it in the natural box—ideally of wood or stone—to contain the integrity of its power.

When you've determined it's time to send your thought-form out into the world—which could be right after you've created it or a later time—here are my steps for setting it upon a chosen task.

1. Tap the crystal on a hard surface with a gentle and steady beat to wake up the energy.

2. Call out your thoughtform's name, loudly and boldly if possible. Imagine the being emerging from the crystal in a beam of light before you.

3. As if you were an army general, belt out your instructions as clearly as possible. Be specific but also keep your statements simple. It is good to have this prepared in advance.

4. You may automatically sense that the thoughtform is rushing off to the task. If not, shout a directive like "go!" and wave it off with your hands.

When your thoughtform has achieved its basic goal, call it back by tapping the crystal again, speaking its name, and asking it to return. If you have ongoing missions for it and will continue to send it out again and again, you can simply store it in the crystal and box when it's not out.

If your thoughtform has fully completed what you think it's capable of doing, it's important to destroy it. Thoughtforms left to their own devices are said to run the risk of going rogue and causing chaotic energy disturbances. To destroy your thoughtform you'll either unmake or isolate its chamber, the crystal. You can do that multiple ways:

Smash it with a hammer and throw the pieces/dust in a living body of water.

Bury it in the ground and salt the earth over it.

Throw it into a fire and let it burn until blackened.

If you're going to be using your thoughtform for a longer period of time for multiple missions across a campaign, send it out for what you need it to do and then allow it to return home to its stone. Thoughtforms typically maintain their power quite well, but if you ever feel one needs a boost, project more light into the crystal while the thoughtform is inside of it.

Conjuring the Spirits of Offense

Just as we can conjure the spirits of defense to protect us and our work, we can call upon the aid of spirits for our offensive strategies, too. All of the methods, tips, and procedures we covered in the defense chapter apply here.

Many spirits—particularly ancestral ones—will work on the defensive as well as offensive side. The distinction is that spirits called upon to go out and do things often have a different feel from the ones we call on to stay in one place and stand guard. Some spirits of offense may be called upon specifically because they have an aggressive nature. Other spirits might be known for their ability to seek things out, uncover things, and reveal them for the magician. The old grimoires of Europe are filled with the names of spirits who root out hidden treasure, find and target enemies, bring back wealth and fame for their conjurer, render an attacker helpless, and so on.

While thoughtforms are created, sustained, and destroyed entirely by the magician, spirits of the land and other realms work quite differently. These entities exist of their own accord and must be courted to work with and agree to help you. Refer back to "Conjuring the Spirits of Defense" for the standard protocols for engaging in an agreement with spirits.

There is a densely populated world of spirits well-suited for offensive work that you can pick from. It may be that one of the most challenging steps is deciding which one to work with in the first place. Let's look at a few of the categories of spirits we might turn to for this particular work:

Land Spirits. Spirits of the land can be all you need if you're engaged in environmental justice, animal rights, invasion and occupation issues, and justice for indigenous peoples and their land. These spirits are already interested in keeping their habitat intact, and some are known for actively attacking those who threaten their space all on their own. Countries like Ireland, Wales, and Iceland know this well, and many construction companies will avoid building in their sacred areas. Land spirits known for aiding the offensive work include the following:

Various species of faerie

Dryads (tree spirits)

Genius loci (the overarching spirit of a place)

Grimoire Spirits. References like the *Book of Enoch*, *Sworn Book of Honorius*, *Picatrix*, and the *Clavicula*

Salomonis (*Key of Solomon*) are some of the famous magic texts that contain spells, rituals, and descriptions of spirits and how to conjure them. Many of the most famous books such as the *Key of Solomon* come from medieval Europe. Often grimoires will not only have lists of spirits and what they do, but also images of sigils to use to reach them and what to do to make them amicable to the magician.

Useful Spirits for Offensive Work

From the Ars Goetia

Andromalius: Punishes thieves and people who are dishonest at the command of the magician.

Astaroth: Can hold people accountable for being too vain and prideful, bringing them down into humbleness.

Baal: Teaches invisibility and the art of becoming cunning.

Barbatos: Heals relationships between friends and associates, establishes relationships between citizens and rulers.

Belial: Distributes high titles and regal positions. Useful for election work.

Buer: Teaches moral philosophies and logic.

Buné: Makes people eloquent and can bestow wealth, both useful attributes for campaign work.

Eligos: Grants favor to the magician from rulers and other important people.

Ipos/Aiperos: Can make people witty and their language convincing.

Malphas: Can subvert the thoughts and mental processes of the magician's enemy and make them known.

Marchosias: A strong fighter who can confer vitality and the will to carry on, a particularly useful set of traits to intervene with before burnout sets in.

Naberius: Can make the magician an expert at rhetoric and debate.

Purson: Reveals all hidden things.

Sabnock: A warrior spirit known for building castles and furnishing them with weapons. Can be called upon when resources are needed for a long campaign.

Seir: An extremely quick spirit who can move from place to place, granting the magician's wishes with great speed.

Shax: Known for the ability to "steal money from kings" and return it to the people, Shax might be called upon to take power from a corrupt leader and bring it back to the citizens.

Vassago: A very amicable spirit who will give answers on the past and future and will carry out many basic tasks for the magician.

Vine/Vinea: Known for destroying barriers and walls, removing obstacles.

It is important to note when working with grimoire spirits, particularly from the *Goetia*, that many of them have very specific ways they must be approached. It is always wise to research the nature and disposition of spirits like this before calling upon them. While many of them will easily aid the magician when called upon, they may also have very particular proclivities for how they ought to be addressed and appeased. Aside from the specific requirements of the spirits themselves, the *Lesser Key of Solomon* gives us various invocation procedures to call them including this one:

> I do exorcise thee and do powerfully
> command thee, O thou Spirit [Name] that
> thou dost forthwith appear unto me here
> before this Circle in a fair human shape,
> without any deformity or tortuosity. And by
> this ineffable name, TETRAGRAMMATON
> IEHOVAH, do I command thee, at the which
> being heard the elements are overthrown, the
> air is shaken, the sea runneth back, the fire
> is quenched, the earth trembleth, and all the
> hosts of the celestials, terrestrials, and infernals,
> do tremble together, and are troubled and
> confounded. Wherefore come thou, O Spirit
> [Name], forthwith, and without delay, from
> any or all parts of the world wherever thou
> mayest be, and make rational answers unto
> all things that I shall demand of thee. Come
> thou peaceably, visibly, and affably, now, and
> without delay, manifesting that which I shall
> desire. For thou art conjured by the name of
> the LIVING and TRUE GOD, HELIOREN,

> wherefore fulfil thou my commands, and
> persist thou therein unto the end, and
> according unto mine interest, visibly and
> affably speaking unto me with a voice clear
> and intelligible without any ambiguity.

....

From the Lore of Angels

Gabriel: Instills mental and spiritual strength in a long journey or process.

Haniel: When things become heated between people (even allies during a stressful campaign), Haniel can instill compassion, understanding, and love between them.

Michael: Warrior archangel who helps us become fearless.

Raphael: The healer archangel who can prevent burnout and help an activist recover from it.

Tzafkiel: Able to put an end to something while simultaneously replacing that thing with something more favorable.

Uriel: Concerned with the material world, Uriel can aid in gathering resources.

Angelic spirits are considered among the safest spirits to conjure, as their primary goal in existing is to aid and advance human endeavors and states of being. There are unspeakably long lists of angels from many sources throughout history. The few I've listed here are some of the most well-known and also happen to have specific attributes useful to activism. If you will be working regularly with spirits, it would be worth it to gain a deeper familiarity with the angelic realms if those sorts of spirits appeal to you.

The old grimoires give similar instructions for calling upon the angels as they do the other sorts of spirits. That said, angelic beings tend to be more willing to come to the aid of a magician who doesn't necessarily have all of the extra trappings of ritual other spirits may require. Angels are known to be favorable to magicians who simply approach them with a pure heart, a clear intention, and a willingness to achieve their goals in alignment with what they believe to be their divine work.

Symbols and Sigils of Offense

As with symbols of defense, symbols of offense can also be worn as jewelry, although this might not be as common since our offensive approaches tend to be used quickly and only for a limited time until we move on with the next stage of our campaign. Symbols of offense will more often be used in petition magic, candle burning, and traced into the air with energy during a specific situation.

These symbols would do well inscribed on campaign materials meant to be received by people involved with your mission goal. I might also use some of these symbols in decorating my workspace and home to inspire me and grant me their aid while I work.

Just as there is a near infinite list of defensive symbols, there are countless options designed to manifest, target, and transform. The symbols below are among the most common specifically dealing with harnessing, focusing, and sending specific patterns of energy out into the world. Many, if not all, of the offensive spirits have their own symbols and sigils, which can be utilized for that specific type of spirit work.

Lemniscate (Infinity Loop). The symbol for infinity can be used to rapidly draw up energy and get things moving. It is an excellent choice for raising power and instilling it within something. It can be drawn over the crystal home of a thoughtform to keep it charged up. It is associated with the cosmos as well as the power of the ancestors.

Triskelion. This common Celtic symbol has mysterious origins, although many agree that it has something to do with the powers of life, death, and rebirth. In modern use it's associated with the powers of land, sea, and sky. Activists might use the triskelion to activate the spirits of the land to come and carry out some important work relating to environmental topics that affect the land, sea, and sky.

Swords. Images of swords can be placed on your person to call upon the archetypal power of the warrior and inspire within you the need to press on and do work that is challenging. It can also be used as a magical symbol to cut through the obstacles standing in the way of victory. Specific sword imagery, like that used in various tarot card decks, might be meditated upon for specific needs.

Mars. Mars is the planet of battle, aggression, and the essence of what it means to get things done quickly and effectively. It is associated with the warrior/destroyer Samael and the ability to burn away those old systems that are no longer useful and standing in the way of progress.

S	A	T	O	R
A	R	E	P	O
T	E	N	E	T
O	P	E	R	A
R	O	T	A	S

SATOR Square. One of many magical squares used in rapid manifestation, the SATOR square is thought to roughly mean "Creator, stop! Reverse, hold, turn." It is drawn and spoken aloud to turn back energies and influences working against you and to make those same energies an ally to your own work. It can cause you to become more influential in your negotiations and discussions when drawn as a charm and placed in the pocket.

Ansuz Rune. Ansuz is the rune representing the "voice of the gods." Commonly meaning communication, messaging, and getting one's ideas across, Ansuz can be an aid to those involved with debate and protest as a means to carry the demands of a campaign to the decision-makers and to ensure that those messages will be seen and received properly.

Victory and Loss

For me, winning isn't something that happens suddenly on the field when the whistle blows and the crowds roar. Winning is something that builds physically and mentally every day that you train and every night that you dream.

—Emmitt Smith

In activism, as with many things in life, you will win some things and lose others. Many activists have very strong feelings about victory and loss. When we lose, some will tell us it's important to do so with grace, to protect the dignity of a movement so that we will be well poised to pick ourselves back up and try again in the future. Others will say that in the work of justice we must always have our eyes set on concrete victories or else we're just changing the feeling of a culture rather than the reality of it. In any case it's worth saying a few words about victory and loss as it pertains to our magical goals and ideas.

Witches and magicians know that victory is not always certain. We study and train and do our best in the hope that our work always succeeds, of course, but that is no guarantee of a positive outcome. I believe there is a fine art to accepting loss and moving on. Accepting a loss doesn't mean that you approve of it or celebrate it but rather that you are acknowledging the space you're in with just enough distance from it that you'll be able to evaluate what went wrong and try again. The relationship between activism and magic and how we handle failure is nearly identical. We serve a passion to our goals and want them to succeed, but we also know that we are human beings with limited resources and space for imperfection.

Victory might not seem like something that we should consider evaluating, but even winning comes with its own set of complications. We should be proud of our victories and celebrate our hard work. But sometimes victory can make us feel too complacent and lure us into a false sense of security. When we are victorious with our magical efforts, we should make a note of it so that we can replicate the successful parts in the future. The same is true with our activist campaigns, and good advocates are always looking for winning strategies that they can repeat for similar goals in the future. Something that might be a winning strategy once might not be an automatic recipe for success in the future, but it gives you a good ground to build from.

Throughout your efforts in both magic and activism, you will not only experience large victories and losses, but you'll probably also experience them in smaller ways all along your journey. Certainly the work of justice and equality can feel like we are taking two steps forward one day and two steps back the next. When we're lucky, it can feel like we're speeding right up through the finish line as well. Because of the dynamic nature of victory and loss it is important that we channel the power of flexibility and adaptability with all things. In our magic, the number one thing that keeps us open is maintaining a daily practice to keep our magical skills sharp and our spiritual selves empowered. In our activism we learn that being resilient is simply an essential element of survival. Even small losses with things we care about can feel so crushing to the spirit and make us hesitant to try again, but having the ability to take the hits and keep on going is an important skill to learn and master.

On June 27, 2018, legendary civil rights activist and U.S. Representative for Georgia John Lewis posted a tweet that feels particularly relevant. In it he advises the reader to "not get lost in a sea of despair." He goes on to say that we should not "be afraid to make some noise and get in good trouble."

Be proud of what you've done when you win. Be proud of what you've done even when you lose. In a world that can sometimes feel so burdened with apathy, know that you are likely doing more than many. In my opinion, simply having the nerve to approach this work again and again is a regular victory in itself.

Spell to Cultivate Resilience

Materials:

Flower heads or petals

Bowl of springwater

Candle

Resilience is a state of being and a skill that allows us to spring back from exhaustion and burnout. Building a sense of resilience will help you avoid wearing down and restore your energy reserves. For this spell, we incorporate basic elemental symbolism. The flame of the candle represents the chaos of our world and its effect on us all. Flowers signify the gentleness of earth and remind us of the beauty all around us. The bowl of water reminds us of the deep well of power we all have within us and that we have the power to calm our troubled waters.

This is one of my oldest spells. I've been working it since my early days in activism, and it's helped to pull me back from the brink of burnout many times. I recommend casting this spell when you feel that your normal measures for avoiding burnout may not be working so well. You can also schedule yourself time to perform it a few times a year to make sure your personal resiliency is always strong.

Fill the bowl of water and place a few flower heads gently upon the surface so that they float on the top. Place the candle in front of the bowl.

Light the candle and stare into the flame. Call up all of the chaos, exhaustion, and overwhelming feelings you can think of, whether relating to your activist efforts or not. Allow these feelings to well up strongly within you, tied to the flame of the candle. At the peak of these emotions, say:

> *The world at times a frenzied fire,*
> *(Blow out the flame and then continue to say . . .)*
> *And I the calm in tempest dire.*
> *Still the waters, calm the fire.*
> *Still the waters, calm the fire.*

As you chant the last two lines, gently touch the flowers and gaze upon them as they glide across the surface. Allow yourself to become momentarily lost in the beauty and serenity of earth and water. Breathe slowly and deeply, feeling your own inner storm becoming tempered into a calm pond, like the water before you. Do this for as long as you like, until you feel awash with the powers of resilience and serenity.

History
and Culture

Myths and Lore

The work of activism is built on the shoulders of giants. Many have come before us and worked and sacrificed, some to the point of death, to bring us where we are today. While we still have so much work left to do, we must honor the heroes of the past if we're to have the wisdom to do this work in the present. Learning about their lives and the contributions they made, recognizing them through ceremony and prayer, and working with them magically are the ways to carry on their legacies.

Most of the heroes of the civil and environmental rights movements didn't grow up with the desire to change the world. Most were either forced into a situation where they realized they needed to act or their great compassion compelled them to do good deeds for others. The women who worked for suffrage knew that they'd need to take action to create a better world for themselves and their daughters. Men of privilege like Gerald Gardner, who we'll learn more about it a bit, knew that fighting the German High Command with magic during World War II was simply the right thing to do. Some accomplished things barely remembered by history, such as Pamela Colman Smith, while others went on to become great beacons of inspiration, celebrated throughout generations.

History is filled with stories of those who stood up against the forces of evil and tyranny. As a child, I was most inspired by the Greek myths that spoke of heroes facing down monsters, angry gods, evil kings, and beasts of all kinds. There are patterns to these stories. In his book *The Hero with a Thousand Faces* (1949), mythologist Joseph Campbell details what he describes as "The Hero's Journey": a series of events that takes place in a hero's mission that challenge and change the hero, ultimately leading to transformation and victory.

Being an underdog or representing a suffering community and then gaining the power or courage to stand up and fight is something many witches and magicians can identify with. Many people are drawn to the occult because of experiences that have caused them to feel othered in some way. It's certainly the case that mystics are often the outcasts of society, with witches being the ones you turn to when you have no other recourse available.

Aradia, or the Gospel of the Witches

In 1899, American folklorist Charles Godfrey Leland published *Aradia, or the Gospel of the Witches,* a groundbreaking book that influenced and inspired many witches and Pagans and continues to do so. Leland claimed this religious text belonged to a group of witches in Tuscany who had survived centuries of persecution but continued to worship the lunar goddess Diana. According to Leland, a witch named Maddalena gave him the book, which he then translated into English.

Aradia, or the Gospel of the Witches describes how Diana gave birth to a daughter named Aradia, whose father was Lucifer, identified in the text as a god of light and splendor. When I first read *Aradia* as a teenager, I was initially taken aback. It seemed overly aggressive for my shy nature, and I didn't understand at the time why a text that was part of the bedrock of modern witchcraft held such shocking imagery. Still, something about it spoke to me on deeply personal levels. It was a text about being a voice for the voiceless, fighting for what you believe in, and refusing to take the abuse of one's oppressors. As a bullied teenager, this message resonated powerfully with me, and it continues to sing to me today.

Aradia is far from the first time the goddess Diana would be associated with liberation. In her role as the goddess Diana Nemorensis (Diana of Nemi), she watched over a sacred grove at Lake Nemi in the Lazio region of Italy. According to legend, a great tree stood in the grove that no one was allowed to damage. The exception were escaped slaves who upon breaking a branch off the tree won the right to fight to the death for their freedom, as well as the position of the current king of the region. Diana's sacred grove at Nemi ensured that political influence was ever-changing, despite the crude battle involved. Diana is also associated with slaves seeking asylum as well as the poor. This isn't only due to her grove at Nemi, but also her influence as far away as the city of Ephesus in present-day Turkey. As a light-bearing liberator of slaves, Diana seems right at home in the myth of *Aradia* as mother of the first witch. Diana sent her daughter Aradia to Earth, where she took up her post as the first witch. Aradia's mission was to instruct the poor and the oppressed in the arts of witchcraft and poisoning:

> Ye who are poor suffer with hunger keen,
>
> And toil in wretchedness, and suffer too
>
> Full oft imprisonment; yet with it all

Ye have a soul, and for your sufferings

Ye shall be happy in the other world,

But ill the fate of all who do ye wrong!

....

The first part of the text describes how Aradia's mission was to teach the poor such magics as "binding their oppressors' souls with power" and even committing acts of violence upon those who enslaved them:

....

When I shall have departed from this world,

Whenever ye have need of anything,

Once in the month, and when the moon is full,

Ye shall assemble in some desert place,

Or in a forest all together join

To adore the potent spirit of your queen,

My mother, great Diana. She who fain

Would learn all sorcery yet has not won

Its deepest secrets, them my mother will

Teach her, in truth all things as yet unknown.

And ye shall all be freed from slavery,

And so ye shall be free in everything;

And as the sign that ye are truly free,

Ye shall be naked in your rites, both men

And women also: this shall last until

The last of your oppressors shall be dead;

....

Aradia went on to be a great source of early Wiccan Gerald Gardner's *Book of Shadows*, especially "The Charge of the Goddess" invocation/poem written by his priestess at the time, Doreen Valiente, excerpted above.

Although scholars and historians debate the legitimacy and authenticity of the origins of Leland's text, Aradia is still favored as a powerful spirit and deity by witches and Pagans all over the world. Since their inclusion in early Wiccan ritual and liturgy, Diana and Aradia continue to influence the work of the modern Pagan movement. Authors and teachers such as Raven Grimassi and Lori Bruno have used the imagery of Aradia and Diana as figureheads of their own traditions. Activist witches and magicians continue to call upon Aradia and her mother Diana as messianic figures of the modern witchcraft revival and for our work to escape the grip of our oppressors and empower the common people with magic. I am deeply reminded of this by one of my favorite passages in one of the last sections of the *Aradia* text:

> Diana hath power to do all things, to give
> glory to the lowly, wealth to the poor, joy
> to the afflicted, beauty to the ugly. Be not in
> grief, if you are her follower; though you be
> in prison and in darkness, she will bring light:
> many there are whom she sinks that they may
> rise the higher.

Aradia's call to action still rings true to this day.

Magical Activists in Modern History

While the classic heroes of folklore and mythology grant us inspiration and a sense of wonder, most of the work of creating change in the world isn't so glamorous. This is where it pays to look at the stories of the people who have gone before us. Even figures who weren't known for their activism but were able to create some positive change along the way can be great wellsprings of hope for our work ahead and powers we can call upon for aid. Figures of magic and mysticism are no exception.

When I consider these figures, I do keep in mind that they all have their own problematic histories. However, I'm still inspired thinking about the persistent relevance of their ideas. It's one thing to put forth revolutionary ideas that fit within the scope of your own time, but it's another thing entirely to have visions of fairness and justice that stand the test of time. As I weave my own efforts for change in the world, it helps to keep an open mind for the future by thinking about how my ideas might outlive me.

Early America: Deism and Freemasonry's Influence

The founding of the United States is not a pleasant history. It is fraught with the horrors of colonization, the genocide of its native people, and the shame and horror of slavery. The consequences of these actions still torment many communities today. Early North America was also a place of deep superstition and fear, as demonstrated by the Salem witch trials of 1692. Persecution appears to be woven into the very fabric of the country I call home.

In the eighteenth century, we begin to see efforts by colonists to escape the rule of the British crown, eventually leading to the American Revolution. The figures of the Revolution were some of the most brilliant thinkers of the time, as well as some of the most radical. Part of their radicalism wasn't just rooted in their political views of liberty and justice, but in their spiritual views as well. Although the religious beliefs of the men known as "founding fathers" remain in hot debate today, many agree that their outlooks were largely secular, and some hold that these secular views may even have bordered on mystical at times.

Throughout the eighteenth century, a spiritual view known as Deism was wildly popular in both Britain and North America. Deism is the theological position that God created the universe and everything within it, set it into motion, and then left the scene. This gives scientific and mystical views alike room to operate. Deism supports the idea that because God is detached or unconcerned with the daily operations of humanity, the laws of nature and even metaphysics play more of a role in the workings of the world. Deism was popular with the alchemists and magicians of the seventeenth and eighteenth centuries, as well as with scientists and political figures. The scientist, alchemist, and astrologer Sir Isaac Newton is among the most famous deists. Political and scientific views thereafter described as Newtonian went on to influence political thought in the old world as well as the new. Englishman John Locke (1632–1704), a political philosopher greatly influenced by Newton, had a great influence on the great early political thinkers in America.

Deism and the Newtonian views of John Locke would find a hold with American founding fathers like John Quincy Adams, Ethan Allen, Benjamin Franklin, Thomas Jefferson, James Madison, Thomas Paine, and George Washington.

These men, fueled by the impassioned views of liberty and enlightenment, included some whose views were mystical if not downright magical. For example, let's look at George Washington, Benjamin Franklin, and James Monroe, who belonged to a secret society still in operation around the world today: Freemasonry.

Freemasonry (or just Masonry) is based on a system of fraternal organizations that aspire to values of brotherhood and the advancement of humanity. As a system, Freemasonry is based on the stonemason guilds arising possibly at the end of the fourteenth century. The society is known for incorporating related symbolism to express the goal of building a better world like the compass, square, and other architectural tools.

While traditional Masonic organizations typically ban debate on topics like politics and religion, Freemasonry's liberal views on personal sovereignty and the mystical symbolism it adopts frequently bring it into association with both. It's thought that Masonry could have developed out of Rosicrucianism, a mystical cultural movement from seventeenth-century Europe. Rosicrucianism teaches ways of thinking and being that fall under traditional areas of magic and mysticism such as Hermeticism, Kabbalah, and alchemy.

In studying the lives of Revolutionary figures like the founding fathers, I think it's safe to say that several of them had mystical leanings. In any case, it's clear that mystical and spiritually liberal philosophies like Deism, alchemy, magical symbolism, initiation, and psychism are woven through the fabric of not just the United States, but across the Western world.

The Nineteenth Century: Romanticism, Spiritualism, and Suffrage

The 1800s saw a major surge of interest in art, writing, science, and the spiritual glorification of nature. This Romantic era was known for intense emotion and reason alike, placing a strong focus on the visual arts and freedom of expression. The radical shift from the relative conservatism of the previous century led to an outpouring of interest in alternative political thought, a reexamination of religion and spirituality, and a deep thirst for civil rights.

To me there is perhaps no better example of a Romantic era activist and magician than the Englishman William Blake (1757–1827). William Blake is considered a key figure in both Romantic and Pre-Romantic poetry and visual arts. A controversial and deeply perplexing figure in his time, Blake's artistic works challenged society's views on war, social class, religion, and love. Known as an opponent to conventional Christianity as well as slavery and colonization, Blake used his mystical art and writings to push his audience toward a more open-minded and compassionate future.

Blake rejected the rigid elements of Newtonian thinking in favor of a more mystical approach to nature, science, and religion. Writing of the wonders of the natural world, Blake beautifully states

> The tree which moves some to tears of joy
> is in the eyes of others only a green thing
> that stands in the way. Some see nature all
> ridicule and deformity . . . and some scarce
> see nature at all. But to the eyes of the man of
> imagination, nature is imagination itself.

Being open about entering trance states, experiencing mystical visions, and practicing forms of sexual yoga, Blake had a very unique personal value system which some might identify as Gnostic Christianity and others might call natural occultism. Many consider him to be an early pioneer of Chaos Magic due to his tendency to piece together various bits of esoteric methodology as it suited him. A societal rebel, mystic, and inspiration to magicians to this day, William Blake is someone to consider when you apply the tools of art and writing to your advocacy.

While figures like Blake used the arts to draw attention toward transforming the world in the nineteenth century, other movements were connecting their interests in the supernatural to progressive change more directly. Spiritualism was a movement and practice that truly helped define the middle of the nineteenth century. In an age when women were considered no more than chattel in most parts of society, Spiritualism put women front and center. They not only had a voice, but had their voices become the very heart and soul of what they were doing. Focusing on direct contact with the spirits of the dead, Spiritualism purported to be a movement that anyone could get involved with as a method of immediate and interpersonal connection with the worlds beyond.

Spiritualism in America grew up in the same area I did: western and upstate New York. In this region of New York known as the burned-over district, Kate and Margaret Fox of Hydesville became famous for communicating with spirits through a system of tapping sounds. The experiences of the Fox sisters in March of 1848 are considered to be the origin of this mysterious religion that persists today.

While Spiritualism is a fascinating field to study on its own, it's even more remarkable when you consider the role it played in early feminism and the burgeoning women's suffrage movement. Being a spiritualist was one of the first careers a woman could have and be her own boss. Those who went into mediumship professionally injected a rush of sovereignty and personal direction into the movements for equality.

Emma Hardinge Britten, a political lecturer who took her talents to the world of Spiritualism and became a major figure of the movement, wrote in her 1860 book *Six Lectures on Theology and Nature* that the spirits taught her to overcome the conservative ideas of her early upbringing about how women should act:

> My Spirit Guides had forbidden the stage to
> me – my pupils in music shrank away from
> the weird reputation of a medium . . . Then
> came the word of power – "Emma, you must

go out and speak to the world." . . . but this last
charge, to wit, that I, a woman, and, moreover,
"a lady by birth," and English, above all, that
I would go out, like "strong minded women,"
and hector the world, on public platforms!
Oh, shocking! I vowed rebellion – to give
up Spirits, Spiritualism, and America; return
to England, and live "a feminine existence"
once again. With these magnanimous resolves
strong upon me one week, the next saw me
on a public platform, fairly before the world
as a Trance speaker.

....

Spiritualist mediums were highly sought after, and many
weren't shy about expressing ideas of morality, compassion,
and equality that they said had been transmitted to them
from the spirit world. This turned out to be a great recruit-
ing tool for suffrage efforts, and several spiritualists ended
up as notable and highly influential figures in the work of
women's liberation.

Amy and Isaac Post were two such figures who took
the Fox sisters into their home in 1848 and immediately
became impressed with their spirit communications. The
Posts came from a Quaker background, splintered at the
time due to harsh disagreements on how involved the
Quakers should be in worldly efforts to abolish slavery and
advance women's suffrage. The Posts believed that everything possible should be done in a worldly way to advance
these causes, and they quickly drew harsh criticism from
Quaker leaders because of their staunch positions. In the
early 1840s radical Quakers met in their home for lectures by prominent activists such as Susan B. Anthony and

Sojourner Truth. Amy became an organizer and leader herself in 1848, joining several other women in organizing the Rochester Women's Rights Convention for which she was chair. The couple continued devoting their lives to both religious mysticism and some of the most radical pushes for civil rights at the time. Isaac also became a well-known medium and in 1852 published the book *Voices from the Spirit World, Being Communications from Many Spirits*, still in circulation. The work of the Posts remained influential as Spiritualism later took root and carried on into the Civil War, a time when grieving families were more in need of contact with the spirit world than ever.

But grieving families weren't just the consumers of Spiritualist mediumship; they were also catalysts for it. Laura de Force Gordon was born into a family of nine children, and when one of her siblings died, the family turned to Spiritualism. Laura seemed to exhibit a special ability for mediumship and took to the practice right away, eventually touring and giving lectures on the topic when she was only eighteen years old. Upon moving to California, Gordon turned her attentions to suffrage and began lecturing on that, shaking up the young state. She went on to form the California chapter of the Women's Suffrage Society in 1870 and gave dozens of lectures while there. Gordon was considered a radical in the suffrage movement at the time, not only for her intense motivation to push the women's liberation agenda, but for her lifelong love of Spiritualism as well.

Of course, no discussion of the topic of mid-nineteenth-century activism and mysticism would be complete without mention of the notorious Victoria Woodhull. *Notorious* is an apt word in this case because Woodhull's views were not only quite scandalous for her time, but she also later disavowed some of them upon further religious reflection. Many of Woodhull's controversial opponents rose up in response to the feminist newspaper she founded in 1870 with her sister Tennessee (Tennie) Claflin. The *Woodhull & Claflin's Weekly* championed views in support of free love, suffrage, Spiritualism, and vegetarianism.

Woodhull became the first woman to speak to a Congressional committee, arguing that the Fourteenth and Fifteenth Amendments of the U.S. Constitution guaranteed the right to vote already, but that women simply hadn't exercised it yet. While the idea of invoking these amendments wasn't necessarily a new one, it gained her a popularity that brought her into the leadership circles of the women's suffrage movement.

One of the most defining moments of Victoria Woodhull's life came April 2, 1870, when she announced her candidacy for president of the United States. Although her eligibility is still debated, it is commonly accepted that Woodhull was the first true woman candidate for the office. Her campaign is notable for listing African American abolitionist Frederick Douglass as her running mate, although Douglass's support or involvement in the campaign remains a topic of speculation by political historians to this day. Just days before the election, U.S. Marshals arrested Woodhull, her sister Tennie, and her second husband James on federal charges of "publishing an obscene newspaper." Her campaign netted her zero electoral votes, and Woodhull herself was unable to vote while she was held in jail.

In the *New York Herald*, she wrote of her presidential candidacy with the full awareness that she'd be brought into public ridicule:

> I am quite well aware that in assuming this
> position I shall evoke more ridicule than
> enthusiasm at the outset. But this is an epoch
> of sudden changes and startling surprises.
> What may appear absurd today will assume a
> serious aspect to-morrow.

As of this writing, the United States has still never seen a woman president.

Woodhull wasn't just controversial for her views on women's freedoms and Spiritualism, but also for other decidedly less progressive views that were later cited as "first-wave feminism." Woodhull was highly opposed to abortion access for women and supported eugenics, a view that enjoyed popularity in both the United States and United Kingdom prior to World War II. Woodhull is an example of a complicated activist, having views that were equally revolutionary and problematic by today's standards. As we'll see with many of our magical advocacy ancestors, we are hard-pressed to find anyone who can be painted with the broad brush of the hero without any faults.

The turn of the twentieth century continued to bring out artists and magicians who would influence both worlds, whether they were remembered for it or not. It is fitting that the liminality of the turning century would produce figures like artist Pamela Colman Smith (1878–1951). Born in London, Smith led an independent life focused on pursuing her passions as an artist and honing her skills as a budding occultist.

Smith joined the British occult society the Hermetic Order of the Golden Dawn in 1901, where she met Arthur

Edward Waite and Aleister Crowley. The group began to splinter that same year, yet Smith and Waite remained friends and associates. In 1909 Waite commissioned Smith to illustrate a tarot deck. First published in 1910 by the Rider Publishing Company, this deck revolutionized the way the tarot would be designed and read to this day. Although originally published as the Rider-Waite deck, many today will call the deck the Rider-Waite-Smith, Waite-Colman Smith, or simply the Pamela Colman Smith deck in an attempt to balance the scales and honor the artist who created these potent and mystical images.

While not considered a major figure in the movement herself, Smith contributed regularly to women's suffrage in England and donated much of her own art to the cause. She also provided free illustrations and designs for posters and toys during World War I, lending her efforts to the British Red Cross. Because Smith was such a private and retiring person, it is unknown if she had interests in other causes or if suffrage was her main platform. As a woman of color, and possibly a queer woman, it's possible she may have quietly lent support to other issues as well.

Smith truly believed that art, whether visual or theatrical, could be a powerful motivator of change by applying the imagination to conjure up whole new realities. In 1910 she wrote an article in *The New Age* magazine titled "Appropriate Stage Decoration." Her own words there allude to her affirmative belief in art as a revolutionary act:

> Those in power have not remembered that illusion is the aim of the theatre. It is a great game of pretence that recalls the time when, as children, we baked stones in the sun for

cakes, and feared the dragon that lurked behind the garden wall, or by the pond. A remnant of that imaginative life we re-live in beholding a play set forth before our eyes. If the illusion is good, we follow it more easily, and illusion to be good need not be realistic. Realism is not Art. It is the essence that is necessary to give a semblance of the real thing.

Absolute correctness in dress or scene does not necessarily give the illusion. Everything must be exaggerated in order that it may be visible across the footlights.

....

Pamela Colman Smith is my favorite example of a magician who some might not call an activist outright, but through her own work succeeded in making her small corner of the world a better place. Smith shows us that while our work might not always make the history books, we can merge our love of justice with our mundane work as easily as applying paint to a canvas. There are many who come to witchcraft for its art, and in Pamela Colman Smith's story it is easy to see the attraction.

Angelica Charm for Women

Materials:

Angelica plant (dried or fresh, any part)

The struggles still facing women in the United States are alarming. From the constant threat of sexual assault and harassment to the gender wage gap—women in the U.S. are still paid on average 20 percent less than men in the work-force—it is particularly challenging for women activists to be heard. Even in activist communities women regularly have their ideas stolen from them and then repackaged by men.

Angelica is a plant traditionally associated with the Roman goddess Venus, although many modern magical herbal-ists will also say it has a tie to the Greek goddess Artemis. Whether we're associating it with the goddess of love or the goddess of the hunt and the sovereignty of women, angel-ica is a plant that can aid women in getting their voices heard, their ideas seen, and their projects respected. There is no doubt that a great deal of societal work must be done to bring fairness and equity to women. In the meantime, angel-ica can help.

Simply carrying angelica on your person or placing it in strategic areas can bring to bear its favorable influence. For magic workers identifying as women or within that spectrum, you can try any of the following actions:

Pin the fresh plant to the inside of clothing or tuck a bag of the dried herb into a pocket.

Grow it in a garden or windowsill in the home or office.

Brew an infusion with the plant and pour it into a spray bottle to mist its essence in the air or on your person.

Burn it as an incense and waft the smoke over your person.

Whisper your need to the root and then bury it in the ground.

The First Half of the Twentieth Century: The Magical War

By the 1920s, after the U.S. and British women's suffrage movements won the right to vote, the fusion of activism with Spiritualism started to wane, along with the popularity of Spiritualism itself. But in spite of the golden days of the movement being left behind for the rapid social advances of the 1920s and '30s, nearly every form and vein of Spiritualism is still practiced today.

The women and men of the United States and Great Britain didn't have much time to celebrate their recent advances in civil rights, however. By 1939 Adolf Hitler and the German army began invading neighboring nations, throwing Europe into the world war that would last until 1945. With a strategy of invasion by land and sea and bombings from the sky, the Nazi forces tore through the continent, committing unspeakable acts of violence and genocide in their wake. It was a crisis that most of the time could scarcely imagine. It was a crisis that called for not only a strong physical response from the world, but a magical one as well.

Recognizing that the capture of Britain would have been a massive win for Hitler and devastating for the future of the country, British occultist Dion Fortune began writing a series of letters to members of her magical order, the Fraternity of the Inner Light, immediately after Britain declared war in 1939. In Letter No.1, dated October 8, 1939, Fortune writes:

> There are certain basic principles that
> transcend all partisanship; these are the
> prerogative of no party nor any nation, but are

shared by all things living, because they are the laws of evolving life. In the light of these spiritual principles we can guide our lives with steadfastness and certainty through all crises, and may know a sense of inner peace and security that cannot be shaken by any circumstances, not even death itself. And more than this, we can learn how best to bring such gifts as we have to give the common weal.

....

In her letters, Fortune guided members through planned magical operations focusing on set visualizations designed to repel the Nazi forces and keep Britain safe from invasion. If you would like to read her letters, they have been published in the book *The Magical Battle of Britain: The War Letters of Dion Fortune*, edited by Gareth Knight, from Skylight Press. Fortune wasn't the only prominent magician doing this work. Dennis Wheatley, Ian Fleming, and Aleister Crowley all took part in some form of the working. The extent that these magical leaders were in touch with each other about the operations isn't entirely known.

While the ceremonial magicians of the time had their own operations, the witches were said to have done their part as well. Gerald B. Gardner, founder of modern Wicca, recounted in his book *Witchcraft Today* that he was part of a group ritual that took place on Lammas Night, August 1, 1940. The story goes that seventeen witches, most members of the New Forest Coven said to have initiated Gardner into witchcraft, gathered in the woods of the New Forest a few miles north of Highcliffe-by-the-Sea. With a flickering lantern placed in the east as a substitute for a fire, which could have drawn the attention of Nazi planes flying overhead in the direction of Berlin, the witches conducted a ritual to implant thoughts in Hitler's head designed to wear down his fortitude and determination to invade the island. Shouting "You cannot cross the sea! You cannot come! You cannot cross the sea!" they worked up a frenzy and created a cone of power that was then launched in the direction of the German High Command. Gardner reflects on that time in *Witchcraft Today:*

> I am not saying that they stopped Hitler. All I say is that I saw a very interesting ceremony performed with the intention of putting a certain idea into his mind, and this was repeated several times afterwards; and though all the invasion barges were ready, the fact was that Hitler never even tried to come. The witches told me that their great-grandfathers had tried to project the same idea into Boney's [Napoleon Bonaparte's] mind.

While there isn't much to back up the details of Gardner's New Forest ritual beyond his own telling of it, he is right that Hitler never did invade England, and not securing its capture is one of the elements that contributed to Germany's eventual loss of the entire war. Readers interested in World War II history will know that the Royal Air Force's determination to fight off the Axis powers in the air was a major physical deterrent. In any case, it is fascinating to think of not only the newly public witches of the time casting a magical assault on Hitler's army, but also that magicians of many flavors all over the nation were doing the same in their own way. The New Forest ritual was so physically and spiritually taxing that several members were said to have died not long after it took place.

On the other side of the Atlantic in January of 1941, just five months after the New Forest ritual, a group of Washington, D.C., residents gathered at a cabin in the nearby woods of Maryland to hold a "hex party" on Hitler. The account was published in a *LIFE* magazine article titled "LIFE Goes to a Hex Party: Amatuer Sorcerers Try Black Magic Against Hitler." The young residents—many of whom worked for the federal government—enlisted the help of occult author William Seabrook after being inspired by his book *Witchcraft: Its Power in the World Today*.

The would-be magicians (we do not know if any of them practiced magic or witchcraft outside of this one special ritual) designed a dressmaker's mannequin as the effigy of Hitler, shouting at it "You are Hitler! Hitler is you!" to establish the magical link. Then, the invocation was spoken:

> Hitler! You are the enemy of man and of the world; therefore we curse you. We curse you by every tear and drop of blood you have caused to flow. We curse you with the curses of all who have cursed you . . . Istan, send 99 cats to claw his heart out and 99 dogs to eat it when he's dead. It will be soon! Soon! SOON!

The rite ended with the beheading of the mannequin. The ritualists then buried the effigy in the woods, noting that as the worms devoured the doll, so too would Hitler's demise be brought about. Did the ritual by the American magicians cause any particular anguish to Hitler himself? We may never know.

The Second Half of the Twentieth Century: Flower Power, Sexual Revolution, and Feminism

With a religious form of modern witchcraft in Wicca and many forms of ceremonial magic out in the open and sweeping the world with popularity, the postwar Western world enjoyed a surge of interest in both mysticism and revolutionary activism alike. Many manifestations of these efforts were quite serious, while others were a bit more for show. Several of these dramatic showy instances of activism took place in my own town, Washington, D.C. One of the major reasons I love living where I do is that we're not shy about using high drama and ritual theater to stage a campaign.

Nineteen sixty-seven was the Summer of Love in the United States and a major turning point in the Vietnam War. Protests swarmed the country calling for an end to war and the return of peace, particularly in Washington, D.C. Activists Jerry Rubin and Abbie Hoffman set out to work the massive protest crowds for a common goal. Using street theater tactics while incorporating the current time's interest in occultism, Rubin and Hoffman organized a ritual to "exorcise" the Pentagon and levitate it 300 feet upward into the air! When brought before the Pentagon administrators to organize the permit, it was negotiated that the Pentagon would be lifted no more than ten feet in the air. Despite the Pentagon's limitations on the levitation, the ritual went on.

Rubin and Hoffman led a contingency of more than 36,000 people from the Lincoln Memorial—where a larger rally of 100,000 was being held—over to the Pentagon where they could enact the rite. The Pentagon took the action seriously. Its leaders ordered all but crucial staff to stay home that Saturday. Police formed a barricade around the building, armed with riot guns filled with tear gas. The 82nd Airborne Division was on call, just in case. Helicopters circled overhead. Roughly 8,500 Pentagon personnel were on-site to meet the protesters.

At the site, leaflets were distributed throughout the crowd reaffirming the intention and declaring what the group was there for:

October 21, 1967
Washington, D.C., U.S.A.
Planet Earth

We Freemen, of all colors of the spectrum, in the name of God, Ra, Jehovah, Anubis, Osiris, Tlaloc, Quetzalcoatl, Thoth, Ptah, Allah, Krishna, Chango, Chimeke, Chukwu, Olisa-Bulu-Uwa, Imales, Orisasu, Odudua, Kali, Shiva-Shakra, Great Spirit, Dionysus, Yahweh, Thor, Bacchus, Isis, Jesus Christ, Maitreya, Buddha, Rama do exorcise and cast out the EVIL which has walled and captured the pentacle of power and perverted its use to the need of the total machine and its child the hydrogen bomb and has suffered the people of the planet earth, the American people and creatures of the mountains, woods, streams and oceans grievous mental and physical torture and the constant torment of the imminent threat of utter destruction . . .

from *Smithsonian.com*

Between 1969 and 1972, the United States began to drastically reduce the number of soldiers in Vietnam until finally pulling out of the war altogether in 1973.

The continuation of the hippie movement of the 1970s along with the continued advances of the civil rights movement not only fused activism deeply into the fabric of America, but continued to embed the ideals of magical revolution into society and produce occult figures who would influence the world to the present day.

Kenneth Anger is one of my favorite figures of this time. He used his skills as a filmmaker and occultist and experiences as a gay man to express his revolutionary views on society while refusing to separate those same views from his education in occultism. As a Thelemite and member of the secret occult society Ordo Templi Orientis, Anger produced such films as *Invocation of My Demon Brother* (1969) and *Lucifer Rising* (1970), which show an unapologetic protest of conventional sexual norms woven into overt occult symbolism and ritual. Anger is an excellent example of the slightly subdued reality of the 1970s, where his work was only appreciated in later years. While Anger was certainly a notable "California trailblazer," work like his would be admired and built upon as occultists and revolutionaries throughout the '70s continued to speak up and bring their work into the public eye.

While Kenneth Anger was busy learning occultism and shaking up societal norms in California, the witches of New York City were laying the groundwork for a radical history of their own. Early notable gay witch Leo Martello took inspiration from the Stonewall Riots of 1969 to become a founding member of the Gay Activists Alliance along with fellow witch Arthur Evans, who penned the highly influential book *Witchcraft and the Gay Counterculture*. Martello wrote a regular column in the organization's newspaper titled *The Gay Witch*. Continuing to focus his work on the civil rights of witches and Pagans, Martello founded the Witches Anti-Defamation League in 1970, which was later renamed the Alternative Religions Education Network.

The coward finds a way out. The brave finds a way in.
—Leo Martello

Martello came into contact with other gay witches of the New York scene, like the young Eddie Buczynski, who picked up a study in witchcraft after reading Gerald Gardner's *Witchcraft Today* in 1971. Martello introduced Buczynski to a vocal and charismatic man named Herman Slater at a meeting of the New York Coven of Welsh Traditional Witches. After Slater was initiated into the tradition in 1972, he and Buczynski together opened up one of New York's earliest witchcraft shops—The Warlock Shoppe. Their shop was renamed Magickal Childe and served as a major focal point of Pagan meetings and advocacy activity in the New York Pagan scene for decades until its closure in 1999.

Back on the West Coast, the 1970s saw an even greater explosion of interest in magic and Paganism which produced some of the most historical magical activists to date. It was during this time that a young UCLA student named Miriam Simos began studying witchcraft with prominent teachers such as Victor H. Anderson, founder of the Feri tradition, and Zsuzsanna (Z) Budapest, founder of Dianic Wicca. Simos adopted the magical name Starhawk and began teaching her own classes in the mid-'70s. Starhawk's brand of magic, mostly grounded in her training in the Feri by Anderson, was influenced by the political activism she fell in love with upon moving to the West Coast. In recognizing that something needed to be created with justice work as a major focus, she and friend Diane Baker created her own tradition—Reclaiming. Today, Reclaiming members continue to come together for ritual, protest, and trainings around the world.

While Reclaiming has its own strong feminist bent due to influences from one of Starhawk's early teachers, Z Budapest, it becomes the main focus in Budapest's Dianic tradition of Wicca, which primarily eschews male deity in favor of female goddess figures such as the tradition's Roman namesake Diana along with Aradia, Aphrodite, and others. Dianic Wiccans don't have protest as a major focus of their work as with Reclaiming, but the push for an understanding of feminist principles has slowly influenced many traditions of the Craft over the years. This has at times taken damaging turns, as in 2011, when transgender women were turned away from a Dianic "women only" ritual at a major Pagan convention in California. Budapest's follow-up statements confirmed her belief that transgender women aren't part of the Dianic movement she had in mind. As a result younger "trans-inclusive" Dianics at the time began distancing themselves from the main tradition to form their own. As we've seen with many movements within activism and spirituality, the newer members of a group outgrowing the rigidity and problems of the older structures continues to be a repeating formula.

The 1980s and '90s, while considered a "quiet time" in the Western world compared to the previous decades, had its own outpouring of issues that many magicians and witches have contributed to. It was during this time that the AIDS crisis swept through the country, and we know that both the witches of New York and the San Francisco Bay Area gave support in not only healing their community members, but in demanding health care reform through groups like the AIDS Coalition to Unleash Power (ACT UP).

Alongside these efforts, the rapidly growing Pagan communities in the United States and UK formed their own spiritual and political organizations to fight for issues important to them, including the legal recognition of Wicca. In the U.S. court case of *Dettmer v. Landon* in 1986, the Court of Appeals for the Fourth Circuit concluded that Wicca is a religion deserving of the federal protections of the First Amendment. Wiccans, witches, and Pagans around the world continue to fight for basic legal recognition in many areas of government and society. Organizations like the Lady Liberty League, founded by American Wiccan priestess Selena Fox in 1985, still work tirelessly for these rights today.

A Prayer for the LGBTQ Beloved Dead

This is a prayer I wrote to honor our queer ancestors and to ask for their help with the work of furthering LGBTQ equality for all. When I say this prayer, I like to dance in place, expressively and joyfully. Queer folks have long been condemned for expressing who we are. Dance is a way to evoke a sense of liberation and freedom.

> *Hail, shining ones who walk between the worlds!*
> *You who play the lyre and wield the double-axe,*
> *I honor your bright hearts!*
> *By every brick in Stonewall,*

by every banner of identity,
by every beating drum,
may you move like a summer storm
all purple with lightning
across every field and to this very place
where we take your vision forward.
Blessed be.

The Twenty-First Century and Today

The generation known as millennials, with easy access to information on witchcraft and magic thanks to the internet, has taken a major role in leading the Pagan communities as they grow into adulthood. The newer "Y" and "Z" generations, not needing to focus so much time on basic religious freedoms, have been able to use their savvy toward building a Pagan future that's safer and more inclusive for all. With an increased recognition of the challenges that people of color, transgender individuals, and individuals with disabilities face in our communities, many have taken on the cause of building movements for justice from within. Many see this as a major sign of a religious movement maturing and coming into its own, while some in the "old guard" deny or deride these efforts for their own reasons. As with all communities, Pagans don't live in a bubble, and the issues of society around us are our own issues too.

As a millennial, I pride myself on being an advocate for youth, and I tend to get defensive when I see young Pagans discouraged by older ones, which is certainly an issue on its own. Starting in the community as a preteen, I have a keen sense of how important it is to foster the engagement of new generations. Encouraging each other is mutually beneficial to all.

The natural next question is, "Where are we going?" As a movement that continues to weave itself into the issues affecting mainstream society, I believe that our push for justice will continue to be a theme across all sectors of the Pagan community. As we've seen in the generations before us, we take up the issues of things that affect us and the people we care about. With the world growing increasingly smaller thanks to advances in technology and communication, it is my own hope that the trend of helping others and the world we live in will continue to be a theme for magic-makers everywhere. If anything, we certainly have a wealth of ancestral inspiration to draw from.

Conclusion

Neither activism nor magic are things I would consider hobbies. They are lifestyles that require us to pour the entirety of who we are into them. It's possible to dabble in activism just as it is possible to dabble in magic, but the magician who can weave these things into the fabric of their very being is doing a great service not only to their own self but to the world as a whole. When we become the magic we are working, we open ourselves up to the limitless pools of power that the witches before us have been drawing on since that first fallen fire was instilled within our hearts at creation.

Therefore, as you continue to do this work or pick it up for the first time, allow yourself to bring these things into your full identity. Know that you are a magician eminently suited for these times. I have always believed that witchcraft itself is invariably a political act. Magic itself is a response to oppression. When we become fully immersed in the magic of who we are, we become a living weapon against injustice.

This work is not often glamorous and lovely. Know that you will stumble and fall at times. Know that you will mess up, ignore the voices of those around you, and let arrogance hinder your efforts. I have certainly done all of those things, and I'm sure that I will do them again in some way in the future, hopefully to lesser degrees each time. I know that my privilege and station in life blind me from things that I am hard-pressed to pay attention to. Allow yourself the space to fail but do not waste time in shame when you do. Set yourself up with a community of people who will both hold you accountable and cheer you on. This is an endurance run, not a sprint.

Finally, I wish I could leave you with the assurance that doing the work of the activist will make you a better person, a kinder person, or help to create a kinder environment around you. While you will see glimmers of this at times, it will most often feel dirty, painful, and frustrating. This is why I urge you to practice resilience and avoid burnout to every possible extent. We need you in these fights.

Every day is a chance to do something. Anything. While we certainly cannot do everything, we can always do something. Considering this, I invite you to meditate upon these words written by Bay Area priestess and activist Crystal Blanton from her 2015 essay "Renewal and Rebirth; My Path to Justice":

> Each day is a chance to make a choice to start over—to renew our spirits and align our power to a vision that we want in the world. My vision is a place of justice—a world that is safe and right for all people to thrive within it. It is the wish I whisper every morning, and the prayer I recite to the Gods every night. It is the vision that closes that 18-inch gap between my head and my heart; my insides and my outside; my emotion and my action; my past and my present. It is the future that I am envisioning, and the moment of rebirth that I am embracing.

Glossary

Alchemy. The mystic sciences of transformation or creation based on magical methods. A medieval precursor to chemistry.

Burnout. A feeling of intense exhaustion or defeat experienced by activists and organizers. Burnout may or may not involve physical/emotional/spiritual/mental illness as part of the experience.

Civil Disobedience. A type of usually nonviolent direct action that involves purposefully breaking the law.

Cone of Power. The culmination of energy generated by a group of magic workers that is sent toward a goal.

Conjure. To call, signal, or draw a type of spirit or power to do the bidding of a magic worker. (Not to be confused with Southern Conjure as a specific system of regional magic.)

Deism. The belief in a supreme being that does not interfere with or concern itself with human matters.

Demonstration/Demo. A type of physical protest, usually with multiple people, that uses vocal or artistic mediums to display a message and promote an agenda.

Direct Action. A type of activism that involves putting oneself into the direct physical circumstances of an issue. (See also *Civil Disobedience*.)

Divination. The magical art of seeing into the past, present, or future. Usually involving some type of tool such as tarot cards, runes, or a mirror.

Egregore. A type of intelligent power born out of the consciousness of a group of people.

Fetch. A part of the soul associated with primal, instinctual, sexual, and basic needs.

Freemasonry. Systems of fraternal organizations that use allegory, symbolism, and initiatory rites to guide members toward wisdom and morality.

Genius Loci. The spirit inhabiting a specific place.

Godsoul/God Soul. A part of the soul that is fully divine, holy, and perfect.

Grimoire. A magical book of spells, rituals, recipes, tables, or any combination thereof.

Hermetic Principles. A set of seven esoteric statements that explain the movement and transformation of energy as it relates to occult philosophy.

Intersectionality. Where two or more issues of social importance meet, cross, or overlay each other. Often used to mean a specific practice of keeping various issues in mind when working for justice on another, seemingly unrelated issue.

Invoke. To make an appeal to something, often with the intention of having that thing draw near or enter a space or person.

Lobbying. Directly appealing to a decision-maker, usually in person, to communicate a need.

Mercurial. Qualities associated with the planet Mercury: clear, communicative, eloquent, and direct.

Outreach. A type of peer-to-peer activism typically based on educating or informing others about an issue and what they can do to get involved.

Petitioning (Magical). Writing a need on a piece of paper or parchment to convey the need to otherworldly powers such as spirits, ancestors, or gods. Typically the paper is burned or otherwise destroyed as part of the petitioning.

Petitioning (Political). Writing a letter, email, or note to a decision-maker requesting some kind of change that benefits the letter-writer or something they care about.

Rally. A type of demonstration where attendees gather together to cheer on a common cause or (in the case of a political rally) person.

Servitor, Spirit. A type of spirit that is called upon and compelled to perform a specific action at the direction of the magic worker. An entity conjured to serve the needs of the magic worker.

Sigil. A type of symbol designed and used for a specific magical goal.

Spiritualism. The belief or practice of communicating with the spirits of the dead. As a religious movement, Spiritualism reached peak popularity between the 1850s and the 1920s.

Suffrage. The right to vote in elections. Typically applied to the women's suffrage movements in the United States and United Kingdom.

Talker. A part of the soul responsible for communicating with the waking world and those within it. The container of our personalities and egos.

Thoughtform. An entity created by the imagination, power, and intention of a magic worker with a specific goal or mission in mind.

Trance. A state of unordinary consciousness, often induced by way of an external stimuli such as sound, sight, or movement.

Ward. A magical shield or barrier meant to protect those within it and repel the inhabitant's enemies.

Will. A deliberate, self-directed purpose or desire. Magicians sometimes use will (lowercase) to indicate an immediate or short-term desire as opposed to Will (uppercase) to indicate the internal mechanism by which a person's needs and desires become aligned with their true purpose or True Will.

Recommended Reading

On Practical Magic, Paganism, and Revolution

Fortune, Dion. *The Magical Battle of Britain*. Cheltenham, UK: Skylight Press, 2012.

Grey, Peter. *Apocalyptic Witchcraft*. London: Scarlet Imprint, 2013.

Rella, Anthony. *Circling the Star*. Olympia, WA: Gods&Radicals Press, 2018.

Starhawk. *Dreaming the Dark: Magic, Sex & Politics*. Boston: Beacon Press, 1982.

Starhawk. *Truth or Dare: Encounters with Power, Authority, and Mystery*. New York: HarperCollins Publishers, 1990.

On Esoteric Activism and Politics in History and Culture

Bebergal, Peter. *Season of the Witch: How the Occult Saved Rock and Roll*. New York: Jeremy P. Tarcher/Penguin, 2015.

Braude, Ann. *Radical Spirits: Spiritualism and Women's Rights in Nineteenth Century America*. Bloomington, IN: Indiana University Press, 1989, 2001.

Goldsmith, Barbara. *Other Powers: The Age of Suffrage, Spiritualism, and the Scandalous Victoria Woodhull.* New York: HarperCollins Publishers, 1999.

Lachman, Gary. *Politics and the Occult: The Left, the Right, and the Radically Unseen.* Wheaton, IL: Quest Books, 2008.

Leland, Charles. *Aradia: Gospel of the Witches.* Newport, RI: The Witches' Almanac, 2010.

Ovason, David. *The Secret Architecture of our Nation's Capital.* New York: HarperCollins Publishers, 2002.

On Activism and Social Justice as Social Sciences

Alexander, Michelle. *The New Jim Crow: Mass Incarceration in the Age of Colorblindness.* New York: The New Press, 2012.

Blanton, Crystal, Taylor Ellwood, and Brandy Williams. *Bringing Race to the Table: Exploring Racism in the Pagan Community.* Stafford, UK: Immanion Press, 2015.

Davis, Angela. *Freedom Is a Constant Struggle: Ferguson, Palestine, and the Foundations of a Movement.* Chicago: Haymarket Books, 2016.

Lorde, Audre. *Sister Outsider: Essays and Speeches.* Toronto: Crossing Press, 2007.

McKibben, Bill. *The End of Nature.* Westminster, MD: Random House Books, 2006.

Miller, Jason. *Protection and Reversal Magick: A Witch's Defense Manual.* Newburyport, MA: New Page Books, 2006.

Penczak, Christopher. *The Witch's Shield: Protection Magick and Psychic Self-Defense*. St. Paul, MN: Llewellyn Publications, 2004.

Popovic, Srdja. *Blueprint for Revolution: How to Use Rice Pudding, Lego Men, and Other Nonviolent Techniques to Galvanize Communities, Overthrow Dictators, or Simply Change the World*. New York: Spiegel & Grau/Penguin, 2015.

On Building Magical Skills Useful to the Activist Witch

Cabot, Laurie. *Power of the Witch*. New York: Delta, 1989.

Coyle, T. Thorn. *Evolutionary Witchcraft*. New York: Jeremy P. Tarcher/Penguin, 2004.

Coyle, T. Thorn. *Make Magic of Your Life: Passion, Purpose, and the Power of Desire*. San Francisco: Red Wheel/Weiser, 2013.

Cuhulain, Kerr. *Full Contact Magick: A Book of Shadows for the Wiccan Warrior*. St. Paul, MN: Llewellyn Publications, 2002.

Hunter, Devin. *The Witch's Book of Power*. Woodbury, MN: Llewellyn Publications, 2016.

Huson, Paul. *Mastering Witchcraft: A Practical Guide for Witches, Warlocks & Covens*. New York: Penguin Putnam, 1980.

Miller, Jason. *Protection and Reversal Magick*. Franklin Lakes, NJ: Career Press/New Page Books, 2006.

Salisbury, David. *A Mystic Guide to Cleansing and Clearing*. Hants, UK: Moon Books, 2015.

Bibliography

Alinsky, Saul D. *Rules for Radicals*. New York: Vintage Books, A Division of Random House, Inc., 1971.

Alexander, Michelle. *The New Jim Crow: Mass Incarceration in the Age of Colorblindness*. New York: The New Press, 2012.

Aradia, Sable. *The Witch's Eight Paths of Power: A Complete Course in Magick and Witchcraft*. San Francisco: Red Wheel/Weiser, 2014.

Barrabbas, Frater. *Spirit Conjuring for Witches: Magical Evocation Simplified*. Woodbury, MN: Llewellyn Publications, 2017.

Bebergal, Peter. *Season of the Witch: How the Occult Saved Rock and Roll*. New York: Jeremy P. Tarcher/Penguin, 2015.

Blanton, Crystal, Taylor Ellwood, and Brandy Williams. *Bringing Race to the Table: Exploring Racism in the Pagan Community*. Stafford, UK: Immanion Press, 2015.

Bobo/Kendall/Max. *Organizing for Social Change* 4th Edition. Santa Ana, CA: Forum Press, 2010.

Boyd, Andrew and Dave Oswald Mitchell. *Beautiful Trouble: A Toolbox for Revolution*. New York: OR Books, 2012.

Braude, Ann. *Radical Spirits: Spiritualism and Women's Rights in Nineteenth Century America*. Bloomington, IN: Indiana University Press, 1989, 2001.

Cabot, Laurie. *Power of the Witch*. New York: Delta, 1989.

Carlin, Emily. *Defense Against the Dark: A Field Guide to Protecting Yourself from Predatory Spirits, Energy Vampires and*

Malevolent Magic. Franklin Lakes, NJ: New Page Books, 2011.

Cooney, Nick. *Change of Heart: What Psychology Can Teach Us About Spreading Social Change.* Brooklyn, NY: Lantern Books, 2011.

Coyle, T. Thorn. *Make Magic of Your Life: Passion, Purpose, and the Power of Desire.* San Francisco: Red Wheel/Weiser, LLC, 2013.

Coyle, T. Thorn. *Evolutionary Witchcraft.* New York: Jeremy P. Tarcher/Penguin, 2004

Cuhulain, Kerr. *Full Contact Magick: A Book of Shadows for the Wiccan Warrior.* St. Paul, MN: Llewellyn Publications, 2002.

Davies, Owen. *America Bewitched: The Story of Witchcraft After Salem.* Oxford, UK: Oxford University Press, 2013.

Davis, Angela. *Freedom is a Constant Struggle: Ferguson, Palestine, and the Foundations of a Movement.* Chicago, IL: Haymarket Books, 2016.

Dominguez Jr., Ivo. *Practical Astrology for Witches and Pagans: Using the Planets and the Stars for Effective Spellwork, Rituals, and Magickal Work.* San Francisco: Red Wheel/Weiser, LLC, 2016.

Dominguez Jr., Ivo. *Keys to Perception: A Practical Guide to Psychic Development.* San Francisco: Red Wheel/Weiser, LLC, 2017.

Evans, A. *Witchcraft and the Gay Counterculture: A Radical View of Western Civilization and Some of the People It Has Tried to Destroy.* Boston: Fag Rag Books, 1978.

Ewing, Jim PathFinder. *Clearing: A Guide to Liberating Energies Trapped in Buildings and Lands.* Forres, UK: Findhorn Press, 2006.

Farrar, Stewart and Janet. *A Witches' Bible: The Complete Witches' Handbook.* Blaine, WA: Phoenix Publishing, 1996.

Fortune, Dion. The Magical Battle of Britain. Hackensack, NJ: Arcania Press, 1993.

Freire, Paulo. *Pedagogy of the Oppressed.* New York: Bloomsbury Academic, 2012.

Ginsberg, Benjamin. *We the People: An Introduction to American Politics* (Full Ninth Edition). New York: W. W. Norton & Company, 2013.

Godin, Seth and The Group of 33. *The Big Moo: Stop Trying to Be Perfect and Start Being Remarkable.* London: Portfolio, 2005.

Goldsmith, Barbara. *Other Powers: The Age of Suffrage, Spiritualism, and the Scandalous Victoria Woodhull.* New York: HarperCollins Publishers, 1999.

Grey, Peter. *Apocalyptic Witchcraft.* London: Scarlet Imprint, 2013.

Hughes, Michael *Magic for the Resistance: Rituals and Spells for Change* Woodbury, MN: Llewellyn Publications, 2018.

Hunter, Devin. *The Witch's Book of Power.* Woodbury, MN: Llewellyn Publications, 2016.

Huson, Paul. *Mastering Witchcraft: A Practical Guide for Witches, Warlocks and Covens.* New York: Penguin Putnam, 1980.

Hyatt, Christopher S. and Lon Milo DuQuette. *Aleister Crowley's Illustrated Goetia.* Tempe, Arizona: The Original Falcon Press, 1992.

Khan-Cullors, Patrisse and Asha Bandele. *When They Call You a Terrorist: A Black Lives Matter Memoir.* New York: St. Martin's Press, 2018.

Kynes, Sandra. *Star Magic: The Wisdom of the Constellations for Pagans & Wiccans.* Woodbury, MN: Llewellyn Publications, 2015.

Lachman, Gary. *Politics and the Occult: The Left, The Right, and the Radically Unseen.* Wheaton, IL: Quest Books, 2008.

Leland, Charles. *Aradia: Gospel of the Witches.* Newport, RI: The Witches' Almanac, LTD., 2010.

Lorde, Audre. *Sister Outsider: Essays and Speeches.* Toronto, ON: Crossing Press, 2007.

Linde, Judy & Nels. *Taking Sacred Back: The Complete Guide to Designing and Sharing Group Ritual.* Woodbury, MN: Llewellyn Publications, 2016.

McKibben, Bill. *The End of Nature.* Westminster, MD: Random House Books, 2006.

Mickaharic, Draja. *Spiritual Cleansing: A Handbook of Psychic Protection.* San Francisco: Red Wheel/Weiser, LLC, Reprint edition: 2012.

Miller, Jason. *Protection and Reversal Magick.* Franklin Lakes, NJ: Career Press / New Page Books, 2006.

Morgan, Lee. *A Deed Without a Name: Unearthing the Legacy of Traditional Witchcraft.* Hants, UK: Moon Books, 2013.

Morrison, Dorothy. *Utterly Wicked: Curses, Hexes & Other Unsavory Notions.* WillowTree Press, 2007.

Orr, Emma Restall. *Living With Honour: A Pagan Ethics.* Hants, UK: Moon Books, 2008.

Orr, Emma Restall. *Kissing the Hag.* Hants, UK: Moon Books, 2009.

Ovason, David. *The Secret Architecture of our Nation's Capital.* New York: HarperCollins Publishers, 2002.

Paxson, Diana L. *Trance-Portation: Learning to Navigate the Inner World.* San Francisco: Red Wheel/Weiser, LLC, 2008.

Paxson, Diana L. *Taking Up the Runes: A Complete Guide To Using Runes In Spells, Rituals, Divination, and Magic.* San Francisco: Red Wheel/Weiser, LLC, 2005.

Penczak, Christopher. *The Mighty Dead.* Salem, New Hampshire: Copper Cauldron Publishing, 2013.

Penczak, Christopher. *The Gates of Witchcraft.* Salem, New Hampshire: Copper Cauldron Publishing, 2012.

Penczak, Christopher. *Ascension Magick: Ritual, Myth & Healing for the New Aeon.* Woodbury, MN: Llewellyn Publications, 2007.

Popovic, Srdja. *Blueprint for Revolution: How to Use Rice Pudding, Lego Men, and Other Nonviolent Techniques to Galvanize Communities, Overthrow Dictators, or Simply Change the World.* New York: Spiegel & Grau/Penguin, 2015.

Rella, Anthony. *Circling the Star.* Olympia, WA: Gods&Radicals Press, 2018

Salisbury, David. *A Mystic Guide to Cleansing and Clearing.* Hants, UK: Moon Books, 2015.

Shesso, Renna. *Planets for Pagans: Sacred Sites, Ancient Lore, and Magical Stargazing.* San Francisco: Red Wheel/Weiser, LLC, 2014.

Starhawk. *Dreaming the Dark: Magic, Sex and Politics.* Boston: Beacon Press, 1982.

Starhawk. *Truth or Dare: Encounters with Power, Authority, and Mystery.* New York: HarperCollins Publishers, 1990.

Starhawk. *The Spiral Dance: A Rebirth of the Ancient Religion of the Goddess*, 20th Anniversary Edition. New York: HarperOne; Annual, Subsequent edition, 1999.

About the Author

David Salisbury teaches Wicca- and witchcraft-based topics throughout the mid-Atlantic region. He currently lives in Washington, DC, where he works to cofacilitate Firefly, a national Wiccan tradition, and head up the Firefly House, the largest Pagan organization in the mid-Atlantic region with nearly six hundred members.

To Our Readers

Weiser Books, an imprint of Red Wheel/Weiser, publishes books across the entire spectrum of occult, esoteric, speculative, and New Age subjects. Our mission is to publish quality books that will make a difference in people's lives without advocating any one particular path or field of study. We value the integrity, originality, and depth of knowledge of our authors.

Our readers are our most important resource, and we appreciate your input, suggestions, and ideas about what you would like to see published.

Visit our website at *www.redwheelweiser.com* to learn about our upcoming books and free downloads, and be sure to go to *www.redwheelweiser.com/newsletter* to sign up for newsletters and exclusive offers.

You can also contact us at *info@rwwbooks.com* or at

Red Wheel/Weiser, LLC
65 Parker Street, Suite 7
Newburyport, MA 01950

269 AMAZING SEX PLAY

Hugh de Beer

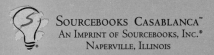

SOURCEBOOKS CASABLANCA™
AN IMPRINT OF SOURCEBOOKS, INC.®
NAPERVILLE, ILLINOIS

Published by Casablanca, an imprint of Sourcebooks, Inc.
P.O. Box 4410, Naperville, Illinois 60567-4410
(630) 961-3900
FAX: (630) 961-2168
www.sourcebooks.com

Library of Congress Cataloging-in-Publication Data

De Beer, Hugh.
 269 amazing sex play / Hugh de Beer.
 p. cm.
 ISBN-13: 978-1-4022-0686-3
 ISBN-10: 1-4022-0686-0
 1. Sex instruction. 2. Foreplay. 3. Sexual excitement. I. Title: Two hundred sixty-nine amazing sex play. II. Title.

HQ31.D37 2006
306.77--dc22
       2005025120

Printed and bound in Canada
 TR 10 9 8 7 6 5 4 3 2 1

contents

ONE | playing with your food

open your mouth and close your eyes...

Discover what flavors and textures turn your lover on. Have them on hand to stimulate the taste buds and enhance sexual desire.

Go to opposite ends of the bed and throw seedless grapes (or popcorn) into each other's mouths. The winner is the one who lands the most.

2 Pass raw egg yokes from one mouth to another without breaking them—great for trust and sensuality.

3 Try the old suck-on-a-string-of-spaghetti until your lips meet.

4 Pass an ice cube from mouth to mouth. Try to do this until the ice cube is completely melted.

coffee, tea, or me

Eat and be eaten with passion.

5 Paint a dinner setting on your body, lie on the table, and arrange finger food for your lover to eat.

6 Put some baking soda onto your lover's breasts and pour Coke over them before licking clean. The tingling sensation is fantastic.

7 Secretly place a dab of flavored edible gel on your body and get your lover to find it just by using their tongue.

8 Lap up your favorite drink from your lover's navel.

9 Work up a sweat and sprinkle sugar on each other's bodies. During and after sex, lick each other clean.

forbidden fruit

10 Take hold of a banana and discuss what you can do with it sexually with your partner. Besides the obvious, you can roll the fruit (peeled or unpeeled) slowly and sensually over your lover's body. After peeling back the yellow leathery skin, the tender meat is extremely sweet and luscious—the perfect fruit for lovers.

11 Scoop out the flesh of a banana like a boat. Pour Irish cream into the hollow and start eating at each end.

12 Pass fresh fruits from your mouth to your lover's mouth.

13 Take a juicy peach or orange and rub it over your lover's bottom. Then sensuously lick or wash the juice off.

14 Dip strawberries or any favorite fruit into chocolate and feed to your lover.

15 Eat some citrus fruit before performing oral sex on your lover. The acid stimulates your own taste buds.

16 Put frozen mango in your mouth before kissing.

aphrodisiacs

Try some of the following aphrodisiacs. Compare notes and discover your favorites.

17 Oats are a sexual stimulant. Feed each other oatmeal with brown sugar, butter, and cream on a chilly winter evening.

18 Curry increases heartbeat, makes you sweat, and stimulates sexual desire. Find the level of heat that works best for you.

19 Garlic has been known to increase blood flow in the genital area. Drizzle garlic cloves with olive oil and roast till soft, sweet, and spreadable. Eat with chewy, crusty baguettes.

20 Lovers find that eggs boost libido. Scramble with cream cheese, add a little caviar, and serve for a candlelight breakfast.

21 Tomatoes are a great aphrodisiac. In the summer, try eating warm, sweet tomatoes fresh off the vine.

22 The herb Horny Goat Weed can enhance arousal and sexual performance.

23 Chocolate is the aphrodisiac of choice. Dip your nipples in chocolate and have your lover lick clean.

24 Buy an aphrodisiac cookbook and transform your dinners at home.

how sweet it is

Your love is sweet—and these ideas will make your love-making even sweeter.

25 Drip chocolate syrup from some height onto your lover's bare body. Have them close their eyes to accentuate the experience.

26 Fill your mouth with marshmallows before performing oral sex.

27 Lick whipped cream from each other's breasts and genitals.

28 Make edible jewelry from food items such as shoe-string black licorice, cereal "O"s, Lifesavers, or pretzels. Adorn your naked bodies and have a feast.

29 Pour cold caramel syrup over each other and have an oral orgy.

30 Fill your mouth with jelly and perform oral sex.

31 Prepare your favorite dessert and place it over your lover's genital area before eating.

32 Pour honey all over your partner's body and lick to your heart's desire.

TWO | we could make believe

let's pretend

Role-playing can awaken your most private passions and unspoken desires.

33 Pretend your lover is paralyzed and undress, bathe, and bed them.

34 Pretend one of you is a baby and the other the parent.

35 Role-play being strangers in a bar and flirt with each other.

36 Act out the roles of virgins making love for the first time.

37 Act out a scene as a newspaper reporter interviewing a virgin, bondage expert, voyeur, etc.

38 Pretend you're a waiter or waitress and flirt with your customer while serving his/her favorite meal.

playing dress-up

39 Rent professional uniforms and then role-play the characters you feel would normally wear them.

40 Surprise your partner by dressing as one of their favorite fantasy figures.

41 Organize a private dress-up party. Try roles like teacher/student, nurse/patient, captor/prisoner, or pirate/wench.

42 Enroll in a first-aid course together and play doctors and nurses.

43 Dress up and act like a highly paid gigolo or call girl.

44 Wrap yourself up as a gift for your lover to open.

45 Design erotic clothing for each other.

46 Wrap a pearl necklace around your hand and roll up and down your lover's genitals.

47 Designate a trunk or suitcase where you will collect exotic clothing and props for your sex play.

imagine that

48 How would you go about making love in an elevator that has been stuck between floors? Try it at home first in a closet or wardrobe.

49 With your partner, make up a survival kit that you could use on a deserted island.

50 Make a list of lovemaking techniques, a list of erotic places to make love, and several different times of the day to make love. Select one of each and carry out the instructions.

cross my heart

Roll a die to see who goes first. Then throw the die again, and whatever number comes up, read out loud and complete the excuse:

5|1 The bite on my neck was caused by...

5 2 Those Valentine's flowers...

5 3 We only kissed, it didn't...

5 4 I got these scratch marks from...

5 5 The hair on my jacket is...

5 6 Not tonight, I've...

THREE | can i play with you?

feels so good

57 Use an ice cube to stimulate your partner's skin. You may wish to use it on your partner's feet, neck, lips, navel or genitals—whatever feels like fun.

58 Drip melted wax onto parts of the naked body. When it cools, scrape off with your fingernails and then run an ice cube over the skin.

59 Spiral your tongue down the sides of your lover's body.

60 Put marbles in a sock and massage your lover's bottom.

seductive sensations

61 Use a soft brush or cloth to give your partner a gentle brush down. Start at the right hand, and brush up and down the right side of the body to the toes. Brush the left hand and work up the arm, then down the body to the left foot.

62 Brush your lover's hair. Afterward, take the brush and slowly work your way from the center of the scalp down the spine to the buttocks.

63 When your lover stands, you might even want to give them a friendly smack on the bottom with the brush.

it's get-up time

64   Wake your lover by licking their spine.

65   Give your lover oral sex while they sleep.

66   Randomly set the alarm clock for different times and wake up to have sex.

67   Perform feather light strokes on your sleeping lover's body, from the toes to the top of the head, working your way around both sides of the body to gently wake them.

68 Wake your lover with a passionate kiss.

69 Make a game of dressing your partner in the morning.

don't stop

7 0 Massage your lover's body just using your tongue.

7 1 Use your fingertips to massage your lover's scalp. Start at the hairline and gradually work towards the crown of the head. Finish off with an outward flicking motion as if you are flicking any tension out from the scalp.

72 Get into the 69 position and massage each other without touching the genitals.

73 Give your lover a massage while telling them what you like about each body part you touch.

74 Use lotion or cream to massage your partner's hands. Massage one hand at a time working from each fingertip through the wrist. Concentrate on the wrist, the back of the hand, the palms, thumbs, the knuckles, and tips of the fingers. Also try kissing or sucking the fingers.

75 Slowly press your thumbs in deep circles from the nape of your partner's neck to the base of their spine.

76 Give your lover a forehead massage. Begin by putting your thumbs together in the middle of the forehead with the palms of your hands resting on the temples. Stroke the brow, bringing your thumbs firmly across the eyebrows.

essential oils

Fragrant oils engage all your senses for a sumptuous experience. Make good use of them in your sex play.

77 Using both hands, rub fragrant oil into your lover's thighs. Start above the knee of the right leg and slowly massage oil up to the groin. When you have finished, work on the left leg.

78 Massage your lover's bottom. Start by rubbing fragrant oil into each cheek, then work your way between the legs.

79 Seek out the tensest part of your lover's body. Use massage oil and work out the kinks. After you finish, it's your lover's turn to work on you.

80 Start slowly and sensuously, gradually working up to a brisk, vigorous massage using both hands. Slap occasionally.

aromatherapy

When fragrant oils are massaged into the skin, your body heat releases the scent at its most seductive and intoxicating levels. Try some of the following.

81 | Delicious scents such as cinnamon, almond, and apple.

82 Exotic scents such as ylang-ylang, sandalwood, and jasmine.

83 Old-fashioned scents such as lavender, rose, and chamomile.

FOUR | getting silly

condom chuckles

84 Blow up several condoms and draw weird patterns or dirty pictures on them with markers.

85 Fill the tip of a condom with a small piece of ice before using it for sex.

86 Use condoms to tie your lover to the bed. Be careful not to be too harsh on the condoms, you might want to use them afterward.

you can't be serious...

87 Place a large sheet of plastic on the bed. Cover each other in oil and try to have sex without holding on.

88 Fill a water pistol with warm water and squirt directly onto sensitive parts of the body.

89 Fill water balloons with different color paints and have a fight while naked. Take photos of the end results.

90 Place your underwear in the freezer for an hour or so before putting them on and jumping into bed.

91 Shave each other's pubic hair into creative shapes.

my o my

92 Devise a way to make your lover reach orgasm using an unusual part of your body.

93 Swivel your hips just before and during orgasm.

94 Develop the skill of being able to orgasm by just thinking about your lover.

95 When you are about to orgasm, start counting down from twenty so your lover can join in. Try building the countdown to fifty and then a hundred.

have you tried this?

96 Using a straw, blow around the genital area.

97 While mounted on your partner, screw from left to right instead of going up and down.

98 Make love while sucking your lover's fingers.

location, location, location

99 Try having sex on a chair with wheels.

100 Going to your lover's work place to find somewhere for a quickie can be very exciting.

101 While out eating at a restaurant, take off your shoes and give your lover an inner thigh massage.

102 The hood of a running car is a great vibrating sexual device that can assist in all areas of sex play.

grown-up toys

103 Place a vibrator under your chin when performing oral sex.

104 Buy a commercial cold pack to bring your lover's body temperature down during sex.

105 Use a vibrator to massage your partner's body; don't massage the genital area or the nipples. Avoid these areas but carefully work very close, and you will drive your lover wild.

106 Place several spiky rubber balls under the fitted sheets before sex.

FIVE | nature games

flower power

The rose is the ultimate flower of love and legend. It is utilized many times as a symbol in mythology representing the Greek goddess of sexual love and beauty, Aphrodite, and her Roman counterpart, Venus.

107 Place a single red rose on your partner's pillow.

108 Weave flower petals into your lover's pubic hair.

109 The silky feeling of rose petals is extremely sensual. Secretly cover the sheets on your bed with rose petals and as you and your partner are making love, the texture of the petals will heighten the skin-to-skin contact.

au natural

110 Spend a week without electricity. Use candles, eat food that doesn't need cooking, and shower in cold water. Discover new ways to entertain and warm each other.

111 Leave the television off for a week and then another time for a month.

112 Spend an entire weekend nude.

113 On a balmy night with a full moon, spread a blanket on the ground and make love in the moonlight.

the birds & the bees

114 Research how different animals attract the opposite sex. Try their methods on each other.

115 Pretend you are your favorite animals and have sex in the way you think those animals might. For variety, select bizarre animals.

116 Pretend one of you is a flower and the other is a bumblebee.

outdoor adventures

Sex outdoors is not only extremely erotic but is also healthy for your relationship. It's important to vary your love making patterns.

117 Try your local beach, park, or woods.

118 Buy a blow up kiddy pool and have a water orgy in the backyard.

119 Go camping! Share a sleeping bag for some hot close-up sex.

120 Go skinny-dipping in the ocean. The salt is good for the skin and the sea is invigorating.

121 Have sex in a hammock.

122 Try having sex under a waterfall.

123 Try sex in a two-person canoe.

primal scream

124 During the next full moon, hold hands with a crystal between your palms and make a wish, then howl at the moon.

125 As a weekend activity, make up different types of masks. Devise some dances and love making techniques that suit each mask.

126 Make homemade musical instruments and invent tribal sex sounds. Record your results.

six | i'll race you

double dare

Challenges and competition will stimulate your imagination as well as your sex life.

127 Become a member of the mile high club.

128 Go to a multi-story building and make love in an elevator.

129 Attempt totally silent sex.

130 Try having sex without using your arms or legs.

131 Put your hands on your head. Get your partner to try everything to get your hands off without physically pulling your hands away. You can take turns but you or your partner must be fairly gentle (tickling included). As a variation use only the mouth.

for the athletic

132 Investigate the sexual possibilities of various yoga positions, including the Bridge, the Cat, and Downward Dog.

133 Workout with your kisser. Kissing exercises thirty-nine muscles, seventeen of which are in the tongue. It can increase your pulse rate from seventy to 150 in one session.

134 Go to the pool and learn synchronized swimming with each other—a great way to get your sexual rhythms in sync.

135 As a form of foreplay, develop some stretching exercises before having sex.

steamy sex

136 Do aerobics together for a half an hour to work up a good sweat. Then lick the sweat off each other's bodies.

137 Do naked push-ups over your lover, kissing them every time you go down.

138 Try mud wrestling with your partner.

139 Learn the Tango and do it naked.

let's play games

140 Make an X-rated version of the game of Clue. Make a map of your house and inside each room write the day, the time, and the sex toy you'll use to commit the deed.

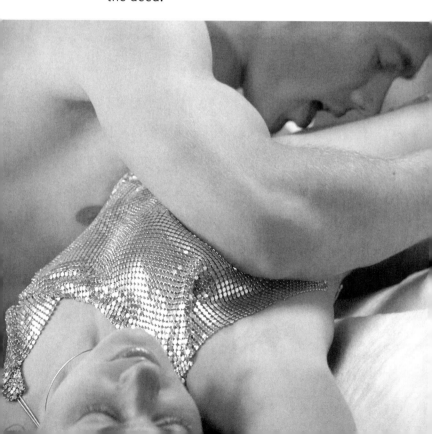

141 Play Scrabble with your lover using only words with sexual meaning or connotations.

142 Play tic-tac-toe on your partner's naked body.

143 Play sexual body charades.

144 Use your tongue to spell out letters on your lover's genitals and see if they can decode your message.

SEVEN | i love it when you talk dirty

tell me a story

Raise your lover's blood pressure with erotic suggestions and naughty words.

145 Buy a naughty magazine and read it with your partner.

146 While in public, whisper erotic ideas you'd like to do to each other.

147 Read erotic literature aloud to each other and discuss your favorite parts.

148 Share your fantasies with your partner. The more you do this the better you and your partner become at understanding your inner sexual being.

sex secrets

149 Slip a note into your lover's pocket revealing your current favorite fantasy.

150 Write your lover a letter describing a new erotic activity you'd like to try with them.

151 Write about the way your orgasm feels emotionally, physically, and intellectually.

152 Discuss with your partner how, if you had it to do all over again, you would orchestrate the loss of your virginity.

153 Discuss exotic places you'd like to have sex.

word play

154 Say a tongue twister while kissing passionately.

155 Recite your favorite romantic poetry while making love.

156 Together, make up a sexy fairy tale, or revise a classic fairy tale to include X-rated scenes.

157 Pick a story that ends with "they married and lived happily ever after" and take turns imagining the characters' honeymoon. Where did they go? What did they do?

phone sex

158 Perform oral sex on your lover while they are talking to someone on the phone.

159 Try a "quickie" in a phone booth.

160 Phone your lover at work and tell them what you intend to do with them when they get home.

161 While your lover is talking on the phone, tease them by stripping.

162 Phone your lover and describe an erotic adventure you would like to share with them.

EIGHT | arts & entertainment

film noir

163 Use a blue light globe during sex sessions to simulate a "Blue Movie" atmosphere.

164 Re-enact a love scene from the latest film you've seen.

165 Imagine you're performing *The Full Monty* in a crowded bar.

166 Go to your local drive-in or movie theater. Sit in the back seat and kiss and hug throughout the first movie. Make love during the second movie.

you're the star

Try acting out these scenarios (as lewdly as possible) or make up your own.

167 She is an old maid librarian and he is a saucy teenage boy.

168 She is a corporate CEO and he is an employee who needs to be fired.

169 She is a frightened lady with a secret and he is Sherlock Holmes.

Try role reversal for variety, for example:

170 She is a private detective and he is a sultry babe.

171 She is a dastardly villain and he is a damsel in distress (tying to railroad tracks optional).

172 She is a priest and he is a supplicant.

hitting a high note

173 Tap a musical tune on your lover's naked body and see if they can guess what it is. Swap around and the first to guess ten tunes has the choice of what sexual delights unfold.

174 Sing to your lover. It doesn't matter if you have a good or bad voice; it's still a turn-on.

175 Hum your lover's favorite tune while performing oral sex.

176 Serenade your partner in a karaoke bar.

sound track

177 Before bed, put on some music and dance naked together.

178 Have sex to the beat of a variety of different musical genres, including heavy metal, opera, and hip hop.

179 Give your lover oral sex while they listen to their favorite music through headphones.

180 Make a CD of all the music that makes you feel good about your lover, and give it to them as a gift.

NINE | variety act

peekaboo

| 8 | Practice stripping like a professional, using many layers of clothing and props such as gloves, beads, and a feather boa.

182 Undress your partner ever so slowly. They could be standing up, sitting in a chair, or on the bed. Go from head to toe. Keep going until every bit is taken off, including jewelry.

183 Undress your lover without using your hands.

184 Sit your blindfolded lover in a chair. Feed them luscious, juicy pieces of fruit. If they can guess what they're eating, offer them any sexual act of their choice.

foot fetish

185 Develop the art of toe wrestling with your partner

186 Give your lover's feet a massage using peppermint-scented oil.

187 Use a soft brush and vigorously rub your partner's feet, one foot at a time.

188 Deeply kiss, suck, and lick your lover's feet after you have given them a long soak and wash.

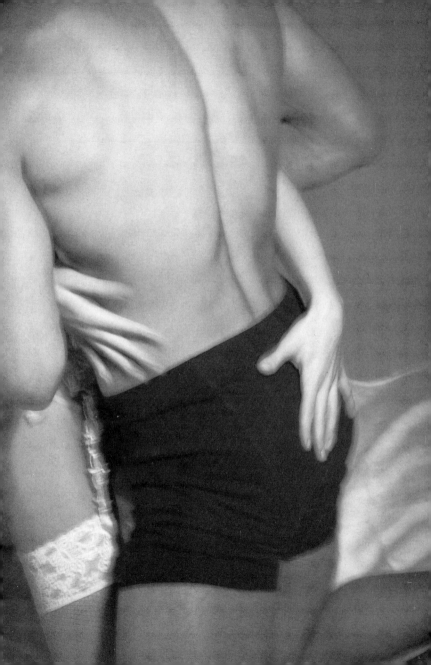

opposites attract

189 Have your lover place a spoon of sugar in his or her mouth while you sprinkle some salt onto your tongue and then kiss passionately.

190 Massage your lover's genitals with your breasts. For variety, cover your breasts with talc and then cover with oil for opposite sensations.

| 9 | Place silk and cotton sheets on the bed together. Now enjoy the ride.

| 9 2 While sharing a hot bath, occasionally sponge each other with cold water.

| 9 3 Share a hot shower, use an ice cube to stimulate your partner's skin. You may wish to use it on your partner's feet, neck, lips, navel or genitals—whatever feels like fun.

tantalizing teases

194 Run your hands all over your lover's naked body, just skimming the hairs.

195 Tease your lover by massaging and kissing around the genital area without actually touching the genitals.

196 Stimulate your lover's body by blowing softly over every part.

197 Lavish tiny licks all over your partner's genitals.

198 Tease your partner by gently biting and caressing their bottom.

199 While out on a date, don't wear any underwear. At an appropriate time, flash your lover.

200 The feather-soft brush of eyelashes on sensitive skin can cause a lover's heart to flutter. Give your lover Butterfly Kisses on their eyelids and nipples.

erogenous zones

201 Lick, suck, and bite the area between the Achilles tendon and the ankle bone.

202 Develop the pubococcygeus muscle to obtain multiple orgasms. Use the Internet to find out where the muscle is located.

203 The nape of the neck is a highly sexually charged erogenous zone. Lick, kiss, bite, and nuzzle the neck to drive your lover wild.

204 Kiss and lightly stroke the inside of your lover's wrists.

205 When kissing, take your lover's tongue deeply into your mouth and suck on it.

206 The arch of your foot is a fantastic erogenous zone. Bite, lick, kiss, and caress.

207 Explore the tender area under the jaw.

TEN | home sweet home

fun with chores

208 Have sex while doing household chores that you find boring, such as doing the dishes, ironing, etc.

209 Put your sheets in the dryer and have hot sex after making the bed.

210 Use a hair dryer (set on cool) to blow all over each other's naked bodies.

211 Auction off sexual favors for getting jobs done around the house.

212 Massage your lover's shoulders while they do the dishes.

213 Hang your head over the edge of the kitchen table while your lover brings you to orgasm. All the sensations are intensified.

214 Invest in a dishwasher, not just for its ability to wash dishes but for its vibrating qualities as well. Explore anything else in the house that may vibrate and include these appliances in your sex play.

215 Use a mini vacuum cleaner all over your lover's body.

weekend delights

2|6 While watching TV, fool around with foreplay during the commercials.

2|7 During a sex session, take breaks to drink water and walk around the house while teasing and tantalizing each other.

2|8 Wear loose fitting clothes often so that your lover has easy access to the delights underneath.

x-rated coupons

Spend a Sunday morning making up your own coupons that you can exchange for amorous gifts.

219 This coupon entitles the bearer to call for an orgasm anytime, anywhere.

220 This coupon entitles the bearer to one deliciously slow strip tease.

221 This coupon entitles the bearer to foreplay *after* making love.

222 Exchange this coupon for a long, wet kiss.

bedroom romps

223 Design a bordello-type bedroom that would turn you and your lover on.

224 Turn up the heat in the bedroom until you are both sweating and then have sex.

225 Put a strip-pole in the bedroom and use it.

226 Position a large mirror in your bedroom so that you can watch your reflection as you make love.

love nest

Walk around your home with your lover and look at areas both inside and outside the house that can be used for a romantic interlude. Assign them numbers and roll the dice to see where to have sex next. Some ideas are...

227 Kitchen: The fridge and cupboards have unlimited ideas with spreads, jams, butter.... Is the kitchen table big enough?

228 Study: Use the Internet. Sit naked with your lover on your lap, facing you. Now see what the Internet can bring up.

229 Lounge: Swing from the chandelier. Put on your lover's favorite video and give them a massage with your tongue.

230 Passage: Tie your naked lover to the hat stand and using a soft clothes brush, stroke all over your lover's body.

231 Bathroom: Pretend your lover is a bath mat and walk all over them. Now wash the mat in the bath.

232 Bedroom: Paint erotic images on your bedroom ceiling.

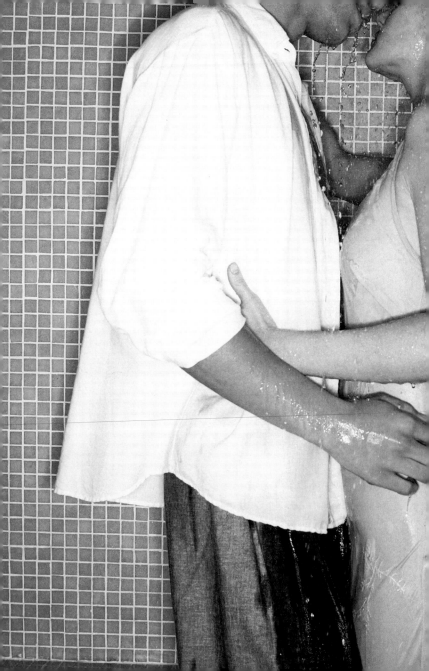

water sports

233 Have a shower together completely dressed and slowly undress each other.

234 Wear rain gear during sex in the shower.

235 Use the flow of the shower water on each other's genitals to reach orgasm.

236 After you have washed your lover in the shower, dry them off using your tongue.

237 Shave your lover's genital area. You'll need warm water, scissors, shaver, soap and a quality skin lotion. After you have finished, get a mirror for your partner to see your work of art.

bath time

238 Instead of showers, spend a week of having baths together.

239 Before sharing a bath, add food coloring to the water.

240 Using soap, leave a love message on the bathroom mirror for your partner to find.

241 Use shaving cream to create a rich lather in your lover's pubic hair. Wash it off with warm water.

242 Run a deep, hot bath for your lover to soak in. Become your lover's slave and follow every order.

ELEVEN | amorous adventures

expanding cultural horizons

According to Eastern beliefs, the lotus plant is linked to fruitfulness and fertility. It is edible, used as an aphrodisiac and has also been used as a remedy for love sickness.

243 To add a touch of exotic fantasy, try sprinkling the mystical lotus petals over your partner's body before making love.

244 Try out a Japanese massage waterbed together.

245 Keep your passport up to date in case you ever take a spontaneous romantic weekend out of the country.

246 Take a romantic, sleeper-train trip to anywhere.

247 Learn the art of Shiatsu, a Japanese finger pressure therapy (find out more online).

248 Study sexual techniques from different cultures and religions.

road trip

249 While on a long drive, massage your own breasts, letting the driver watch. It's a great way to stay awake.

250 While your lover is driving, gently massage their genitals.

251 | Tape-record the sounds of your love making and leave the tape in the car for your lover. The sounds of a couple making love can be very erotic.

252 | Whisper sexy ideas into your lover's ear while driving in the car.

253 | Next time you are stuck in a traffic jam, sexually stroke and tease each other. It's a great way to pass time.

254 Leave a bottle of your favorite wine and two glasses in the trunk of your car—you never know.

255 Stick a passionate note behind the sun visor of the car for your lover to find.

256 Try making love in the front seat of your car, then the back seat. Then start the car and try it on the back hood. Discuss with your partner which position gave you the most pleasure.

shopping spree

257 Find a seductive present for your lover somewhere other than a sex shop. Look for a gift from the heart, not necessarily just a novelty.

258 Of course, novelties can be loads of fun. Look for edible undies (for either or both of you), peekaboo panties and bras, black leather or rubber catsuits and corsets.

259 Look online for an enormous variety of sexy toys, books, and clothing.

260 Shop for a new and exotic scent for your partner. Go together and try on different scents, getting each other's reactions.

261 Next time you go clothes shopping, share a changing booth.

262 Go together to a gourmet food store and take turns choosing the most sensuous foods for a lover's picnic. Consider a variety of cheeses, olives, pâté or dip, fruit, bread, chocolates, or whatever delights you.

getting to know you

263 Close your eyes and trace your partner's facial features with your fingertips.

264 Guide your lover's hands all over your naked body. Explain what pressure you like at points of interest. This will help your lover understand where and how you like being touched.

265 Imagine the first time you made love and tell the whole story to your lover, describing how you truly felt.

266 Sit facing your partner for a few minutes, holding both hands. Try to imagine a flow of energy passing through your hands, up your arms, and into each other's bodies.

267 Moan your lover's name when they go down on you.

268 Any time you want to feel connected, lie in your lover's arms for a few minutes and listen to their heartbeat. If they are relaxed, the heart beat will be slow and steady.

269 What happens to their heartbeat when you start kissing and caressing different parts of your lover's body? Listen for the effect of your caresses.

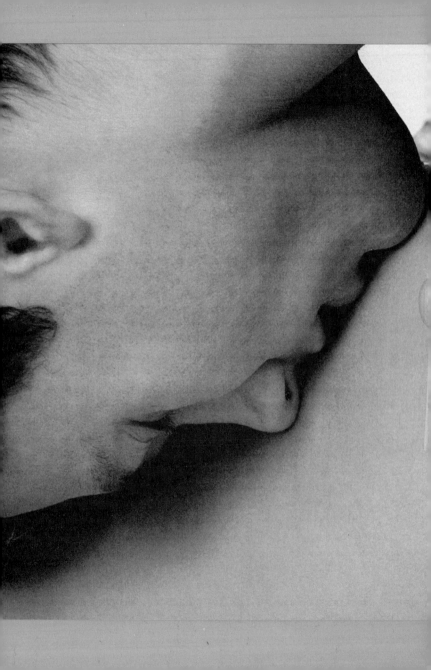

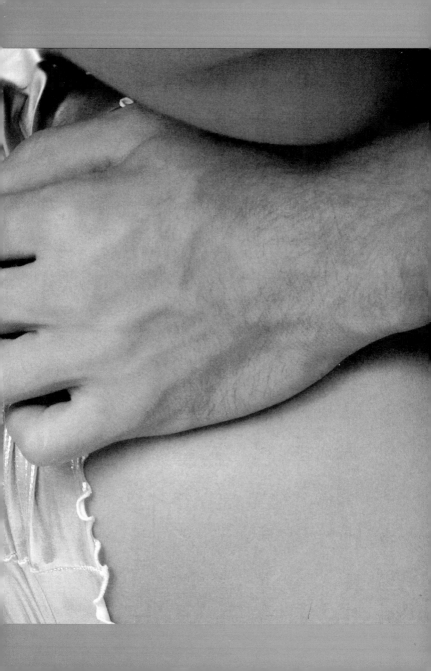

about the author

Hugh de Beer is the creator of the popular *Foreplay* board game (over 200,000 sold). He has written five books, which are bestsellers in Australia, where he lives and works.